Reinvention

*How to Make the Rest of Your Life
the Best of Your Life*

BRIAN TRACY

AMACOM

AMERICAN MANAGEMENT ASSOCIATION

New York • Atlanta • Brussels • Chicago • Mexico City • San Francisco
Shanghai • Tokyo • Toronto • Washington, D.C.

Special discounts on bulk quantities of AMACOM books are available to corporations, professional associations, and other organizations. For details, contact Special Sales Department, AMACOM, a division of American Management Association, 1601 Broadway, New York, NY 10019.
Tel: 212–903–8316. Fax: 212–903–8083.
E-mail: specialsls@amanet.org
Website: www.amacombooks.org/go/specialsales
To view all AMACOM titles go to:
www.amacombooks.org

This publication is designed to provide accurate and authoritative information in regard to the subject matter covered. It is sold with the understanding that the publisher is not engaged in rendering legal, accounting, or other professional service. If legal advice or other expert assistance is required, the services of a competent professional person should be sought.

Library of Congress Cataloging-in-Publication Data

Tracy, Brian.
   Reinvention : how to make the rest of your life the best of your life / Brian Tracy.
       p.   cm.
   Includes index.
   ISBN-13: 978-0-8144-1346-3
   ISBN-10: 0-8144-1346-3
   1. Self-actualization (Psychology)   2. Life skills   3. Change.
4. Success.   I. Title.
BF637.S4T73   2009
650.1—dc22

                                                        2008045967

Printing number

10 9 8 7 6 5 4 3 2 1

This book is fondly dedicated to my friends and partners, John McClelland and Bill Rowland, who have done more to help people reinvent themselves in a positive way than anyone I know.

CONTENTS

THE SUBJECT OF REINVENTION is very dear to my heart. When I was 21 and working as a construction laborer, getting up at 5:00 a.m. in the middle of a cold winter and taking three buses to work all day carrying building materials from place to place, I had a revelation that changed my life. I realized that I was responsible for myself and for everything that happened to me.

Sitting in my little one-room apartment, it was like a flashbulb going off in my face. Imagine! I was responsible. Anything I ever wanted to accomplish from that day forward was completely up to me. No one was going to do it for me.

At that moment, I decided to put my past behind me and reinvent myself for the first time. I looked as far into the future as I could and asked, "What do I *really* want to do with my life?"

Of course, I wanted all the usual things: A job that paid well doing something that I enjoyed, happy relationships, good health, and eventually, financial independence.

I remember going to a bookstore on my lunch break from my construction job and buying books on subjects that

I thought would be helpful to me. I started with business books, then books on psychology, philosophy, economics, and personal success. Because I was single, I had lots of time on my hands, so I spent hours each night reading and underlining.

The more I learned, the more my confidence grew. I began writing letters to companies applying for white-collar jobs. For a long time, I got no responses, but eventually someone hired me in direct sales of office products. That was my start.

Over the years, I have reinvented myself in different jobs and in different industries, moving up through sales into sales management and eventually the vice president of an international company with the responsibility of developing six countries. Later, I got a real estate license and reinvented myself as a real estate developer, reading books, finding financial partners, and ultimately developing more than 100 million dollars of real estate over the years.

I reinvented myself as an importer and a distributor, bringing in a complete line of Japanese cars and setting up 65 dealerships to sell tens of millions of dollars worth of automobiles.

At each stage of reinvention, I sat down with a blank sheet and made a decision about my next step or next career. Then I went out and read books and articles, interviewed people and asked questions, explored the business industry as much as I could, and plunged in.

What I learned about reinvention was that it does not proceed in a long, straight line. There are numerous setbacks and difficulties, and even temporary failures. What seems to be a good course of action often turns out to be a dead end, but something else always appears in a different direction.

I learned that the key to reinvention is to go onto the "continuous offensive." Get a good idea of where you want to go and take action. Try, try again, and try once more. Never give up. Keep moving forward.

In this book, you learn some of the most helpful thinking tools ever discovered to enable you to save months and even years of your life in reinventing yourself and becoming the kind of person you always wanted to be.

Brian Tracy

Your World in Transition

*"*Wherever we are, it is but a stage on the way to somewhere else, and whatever we do, however well we do it, it is only a preparation to do something else that shall be different.*"*

—ROBERT LOUIS STEVENSON, SCOTTISH NOVELIST AND POET

LET THE GOOD TIMES ROLL!

The future may be uncertain, but as you read this book, one thing I can assure you of is that the rest of your life is going to be the best of your life. Whatever you have accomplished up to now is merely a shadow of what you will be able to achieve in the exciting months and years ahead. Understand and take comfort in knowing that whatever changes are taking place in your life today, they are part of a larger plan to lead you onward and upward to fulfilling your potential.

ALBERT EINSTEIN was teaching at Princeton University and had just administered an exam to an advanced class of physics students. On the way back to his office, the teaching assistant carrying the exams asked him, "Dr. Einstein, wasn't this the same exam that you gave to this same class last year?"

Dr. Einstein responded, "Yes, it was."

The teaching assistant, in awe of perhaps the greatest physicist of the twentieth century, then asked, "Excuse me for asking, Dr. Einstein. But how could you give the same exam to the same class two years in a row?"

Einstein replied simply, "The answers have changed."

At that time, in the world of physics, with new breakthroughs and discoveries, the answers were changing at such a rapid rate that the same exam could be given two years in a row and have different answers.

How does this relate to you? The answers in your own life are changing more rapidly today than ever before. If someone were to ask, "What was your biggest problem or goal a year ago?" you probably wouldn't even know the answer. The answers have changed so completely.

Researchers at Harvard University once made three predictions about the future. First, they said, there will be more change in the coming year than ever before. Second, there will be more competition in the coming year than ever before. And third, there will be more opportunities in the coming year in your field, whatever it is, than ever before.

But the opportunities will be different than the opportunities and activities of today.

Those Harvard researchers made these predictions in 1952. They are as true today as they were then. And today, once again, the answers have changed.

Here is another prediction: Within the next two years, 72 percent of people working today will be in different jobs in the same or different companies and have different responsibilities requiring different talents and skills to achieve different results. And those people who fail to respond to the challenges of change will be most affected by it.

Because of our fast-moving society, almost everyone is in a state of transition in one or more areas of life all the time. This rapid rate of change is inevitable, unavoidable, and unstoppable. Knowing how to deal with change effectively is a primary requirement for living successfully in perhaps the most exciting time in all of human history.

CHANGING JOBS

Perhaps the most common form of change is the loss or change of a job. Because of the dynamism of the American economy, fully 20 million jobs are lost or restructured each year. The good news is that 22 million more jobs are created each year as well.

No matter how many hundreds of thousands of new workers flood into the job market each year, the economy continues to create opportunities for them. According to the

Department of Labor, there are now more than 100,000 job categories in the United States and many subcategories within that number.

You could be in transition today because of a career change. After all, the average person starting work today will have an average of 11 full-time jobs lasting two years or more, and five or more multiyear careers in different fields.

It is quite common for people to move from one industry to another and from one part of the country to another, to enter a new job. Many people are changing their professions completely. Perhaps the fun or thrill of a particular job, career, or profession has gone and the individual decides to make a major change. Often, because of changing economic conditions, consumer tastes, and national or international competition, entire industries are downsized or eliminated. The demand for people within a particular job classification or career may decline or even disappear within a few short years.

JOBS AND INDUSTRIES BECOME OBSOLETE

At the beginning of the twentieth century, buggy manufacturing and horse care were major industries employing hundreds of thousands of people. When the automobile was first invented, it was seen as a passing fad. But within a few years, the horse and buggy, and all the jobs associated with those industries, faded into history. Meanwhile, hundreds of thousands—and eventually millions—of new jobs were created in the automobile manufacturing and parts industries. Those jobs were cleaner, higher paying, and offered greater opportunities for advancement and higher standards of living than ever before.

In 1990, one of the largest workforces in America was bank employees. But with the dawn of the computer and Internet age, and the advent of the ATM, fewer and fewer bank employees were required. Millions were laid off and made available to work at more interesting, higher-paying jobs in other industries.

During the real estate boom of 2004–2007, hundreds of thousands of people poured into the real estate, mortgage, and title insurance businesses, many of them earning a lot of money in a short amount of time.

But as always happens, the economy changed. The number of attractive long-term jobs full of opportunities to earn high incomes declined precipitously, leaving many people shaking their heads, worse off than before, and wondering what had happened.

LIFESTYLE CHANGES NEVER STOP

Many people go through dramatic changes in the different stages of family formation. Getting married, especially for the first time, requires a major shift in priorities in many areas of life. Getting divorced, especially when children are involved, can require another major set of transitions. The death of a spouse, unexpected or not, often requires that a person change many other aspects of his or her life.

The birth of children and the entry into family life requires a transition as well. At each stage of a child's growth and development, parents have to adjust and adapt to new pressures and responsibilities. Later in life, when children grow up and leave home, even more transitions are necessary. Sometimes, empty nesters decide that this is an opportunity to change their lives completely, and they do.

Throughout your life, financial changes—especially reversals and even bankruptcy—can require you to change your life in major and minor ways. Sometimes, a major financial loss will require you to completely reevaluate almost every other part of your life.

The rate of change, driven by information explosion, new technologies, and competition of all kinds, is not going to slow down. Knowledge, technology, and competition seem to multiply, increasing the speed of change to almost breathtaking levels.

To ensure that your life stays on a trajectory of increasing success, your goal should be to become a master of change rather than a victim of change. Use these unavoidable and inevitable transition periods in your life to step back and reinvent yourself for the months and years ahead.

THINK ABOUT THE FUTURE

One characteristic of the most successful and happy people is that they are intensely future-oriented. They think about the future most of the time. They refuse to dwell on what has happened and things that cannot be changed. Instead they focus on factors that are under their control and actions they can take to create the kind of future they desire.

Future-oriented people have a special attitude. They believe that their happiest moments and most satisfying experiences lie in the future, waiting to be created or enjoyed. They look forward to the future like a child looks forward to Christmas: "I can hardly wait!"

We are living in the very best time in all of human history. It has never been more possible for more people to earn more money, enjoy higher standards of living, and live longer, healthier lives than it is today. And if anything, these conditions will only improve in the years ahead.

The average life span in America today is about 80 years. As people become more knowledgeable and sensible about health habits, diet, nutrition, and exercise, they can comfortably expect to beat the averages and live to be 90 or even 100 years old in good health.

THE NEW 65

Many people approaching their fifties or sixties are worried about not having enough money set aside to retire comfortably. But don't worry. Today, 75 is the new 65. The average person today is often in excellent mental and physical condition at the age of 65. The average person can look forward to working productively and profitably for another five or 10 years.

A person who is 50 years old today is only halfway through his productive work life. You have more time than you think. This is all the more reason for you to examine your life and begin thinking about reinventing yourself for the decades ahead.

THE TURNING POINT

In a study done some years ago, 300 men and women who had successfully transitioned into new career fields during their thirties and forties were asked a series of questions about their lives. One of the questions was, "What was the turning point between your previous life, which was mostly average performance at an average job, and the extraordinary success that you have enjoyed in recent years?"

All but one of the 300 successful people admitted that the turning point in their lives was "unexpectedly losing a job."

They had been living their lives without incident, comfortably doing a particular job, earning a satisfactory amount, organizing their lifestyles around their incomes, and putting in their time year by year. Then something unexpected happened. It could have been a merger, an acquisition, a bankruptcy, a dramatic decline in demand for a company's products or services, or even a personality conflict with a boss. Suddenly, their job was over and there they were, out on the street. At this point, they each asked themselves, "What do I really want to do with my life?"

Often they had some time to think and some financial resources put aside in the form of severance or savings. They had the courage to look into the future and think about what they wanted to do that was different from the past.

"Unexpectedly losing a job" became the turning point for these people and for many others as well. When you look back at your life, you may recognize that unexpectedly losing a job was the trigger for a major career or life change for you, too. In retrospect, you may look back to that change with gratitude, thankful that it took place, even though it was unexpected and possibly disturbing at the time.

ADAPT, ADJUST, RESPOND

Charles Darwin said, "Survival goes not necessarily to the most intelligent or the strongest of the species, but to the one that is the most adaptable to change."

Your ability to stand back and take a long look at your life, and then to reinvent yourself, can so dramatically improve your health, happiness, and level of satisfaction that it may be one of the most important things that you ever do.

In the pages ahead, I will take you through a step-by-step process of reinvention that you can use at any stage of your life and return to for reference when your life changes again, as it inevitably will.

CHAPTER ONE

You Are Remarkable

"We can accomplish almost anything within our ability if we but think we can."

—GEORGE MATTHEW ADAMS, COLUMNIST, AUTHOR, AND PUBLISHER

YOU ARE A REMARKABLE PERSON who has extraordinary qualities. You have more talent and abilities than you could use in 100 lifetimes. What you can do with your life from this day forward is limited only by your own imagination.

Your brain contains about 100 billion neurons, each of which is connected to as many as twenty thousand other cells in a complex network of ganglia and dendrites. This means that the possible thoughts and combinations of thoughts that you could think would be equal to the number one followed by eight pages of zeros; this number is greater than all the molecules in the known universe.

Dr. Wayne Dyer, a well-known author and speaker on the topic of self-development, says, "Each child comes into the world with 'secret orders'." This means that you were born with a unique destiny at a certain time and place, under certain circumstances, in a special situation. You are put on this earth to do something wonderful with your life, something that no one else but you can do.

You are unique in every sense. There is no one in the world, in all of human history, with the special combination of talents, abilities, knowledge, experience, insights, feelings, desires, ambitions, hopes, or dreams that you have. And there never will be.

Your greatest satisfaction and joy in life will come when you have the wonderful feeling that you are realizing your full potential and becoming everything you are capable of becoming. The only question is, "Are you an optimist or a pessimist?" Do you see the glass as half full or half empty?

THE HIGHEST-PAID WORK

What is the highest-paid, most important work in America? Some people think that the answer is sports, show business, Fortune 500 CEO, or something else. The fact is that the most important work of all is "thinking."

The better you think, the better decisions you make. The better decisions you make, the better actions you take.

The better actions you take, the better results you get. In the long run, and in the short run, the quality of your thinking largely determines the quality of your life. All truly successful, happy people are good thinkers.

Consequences are one of the reasons that thinking is so important. Something is important when it has serious potential consequences, positive or negative. Something is unimportant when it has few or no consequences at all.

The quality of your thinking is largely measured by your ability to first think about the likely consequences of doing or not doing something and then to spend most of your time and effort on those activities with the most significant potential consequences.

A particular quality of future-oriented people is that they think long term. They project forward days, weeks, months, and even years and carefully consider the likely consequences of a particular course of action before they do anything.

The greater clarity you have with regard to where you want to end up sometime in the future, the better decisions you can make in the present and the more likely is it that you will achieve the kind of results that you really want.

Today, you are essentially a knowledge worker. The greater the quality and quantity of knowledge that you have acquired, the more tools you will have at your disposal to shape your thinking, hone your decisions, and ensure that you get better results. Fortunately, thinking critically is a learnable skill. You can get better at it by doing it more often.

THINKING SKILLS FOR THE TWENTY-FIRST CENTURY

There are a series of thinking skills that you must master in order to succeed in a world of turbulence and rapid change. I call them the Seven Rs.

1. *Reevaluating.* This occurs when you take a time-out to reexamine all the details of your life, especially when your life has changed dramatically. You'll know it is time to reevaluate when you experience stress, resistance, frustration, failure, disappointment, or difficulties of any kind. When you are chronically irritable, angry, or unhappy with your work or personal situation, it's a sign that it's time for you to stand back and reevaluate the situation based on the way it is today.

Jack Welch once said that the most important leadership principle is the "Reality Principle." He defined it as, "seeing the world as it is, not as you wish it would be." Jack Welch was famous for going into problem-solving meetings and asking immediately, "What's the reality?"

Strong people confront reality head-on. They are more concerned with what's right than who's right, or being right. They are adamant about finding out the truth of a situation and confronting the reality of their problems rather than avoiding them or hoping that they will go away. They continually reevaluate their situations based on the current reality.

2. *Rethinking.* The quality of your thinking is largely determined by the quantity of the information you have with which to work. In rethinking, you make every effort, as

Harold Geneen of ITT said, to "get the facts." You ask as many questions as you possibly can about the person, problem, or situation so that you can make your decisions based on fact rather than emotions.

One of the best ways to remain calm and keep your mind clear is to ask questions. What exactly has happened? How did it happen? When did it happen? Who is involved? What is likely to happen as a result of this situation? What can be done immediately to address the situation or minimize the cost?

Another way to help you to rethink more clearly is for you to write down every detail of the situation on a piece of paper. Something wonderful seems to happen between the head and the hand. The more details you write, the more calm, clear, and effective you become. Very often, the right course of action will jump off the page at you.

3. *Reorganizing.* The purpose of organizing any personal or business situation is to ensure the smoothest possible functioning. As time, people, and situations change, especially in a turbulent world, you must carefully and continually examine your current ways of living, working, and doing business. Be prepared to organize and reorganize processes, procedures, and activities to increase the smoothness of operations and the efficiency of your work or personal life.

In times of transition, many people reorganize their lives completely. They move from the city to the country or vice versa. They move from a residential home to a condominium, or the other way around. They reorganize their businesses or their personal lives so that they operate better in the new reality.

4. *Restructuring.* Because there is never enough time or money for everything that you want to be, have, and do, you must economize. Restructuring involves moving time, money, and resources away from lower-value areas of activity to higher-value areas.

In business, you restructure by moving your best talents and resources to your areas of greatest opportunity. In your personal life, you restructure by spending more of your personal time on those activities that give you the greatest happiness and satisfaction. This may involve a resolution to focus on the top 20 percent of your work activities, those that account for most of your income, so you can free up more time to spend with your family or on personal activities.

5. *Reengineering.* This popular management tool is aimed at simplification, continually looking for ways to reduce the complexity or number of steps in any process.

You can reduce complexity by delegating low-value, no-value tasks and activities to other people who earn a lower hourly rate than you do or who can do it more cheaply or better than you.

You can reengineer your life by outsourcing all work that is not central to your business or your life and in which another company or individual specializes. Outsourcing low-value tasks to specialized companies is actually cheaper and yields better results than doing it yourself.

Another way to simplify your work is called "responsibility expansion by job consolidation." This means that you bring several jobs together and do them all yourself or make them the responsibility of a single person rather than having parts of the job done by a variety of individuals.

A final way to reengineer your life, to simplify your activities dramatically, is to simply eliminate certain activities and tasks altogether. There are many things that you do each day that may have been important at one time, but now, in comparison to other uses of time, they are of little or no value.

6. *Reinventing.* This is one of the most exciting and revolutionary ways of thinking you will ever learn. Reinventing yourself involves drawing a line under your past and imagining what you would or could do if you were starting over today, in any area, with a clean slate.

If your business burned to the ground overnight and you had to start it over again in new premises, what would you start up immediately, and what would you never start up again?

If your job, business, industry, or area of specialization disappeared, collapsed, or became illegal and you had to start your work life over again completely, what sort of work would you choose to do? Where would you choose to do it? What new skills or abilities would you choose to develop? If you could reinvent your life completely, how would it be different from today?

Practice *zero-based thinking* in every area of your life. Ask, "Is there anything that I am doing today that, knowing what I now know, I would not start up again today if I had to do it over?" This is one of the most effective reinvention tools. I call it a KWINK (Knowing What I Now Know) analysis.

Knowing what you now know, is there any relationship, personal or business, that you would not get into again today if you had it to do over? Knowing what you know

now, is there any part of your business, any product or service, or any process, procedure, or expenditure, that you would not start up again today if you had it to do over?

Finally, is there any investment of time, money, or emotion in your life that, knowing what you now know, you wouldn't get into again? Imagine you could wave a magic wand and reinvent any part of your life from the beginning. What changes would you make? What would you do differently?

7. *Regaining Control.* When you experience a major change or a transition in your life, you may often feel like a small boat that has just hit a squall. You sometimes feel as if you are being pitched up and down physically and emotionally. In the midst of turmoil you will sometimes revert to the "fight or flight" reaction, alternately wanting to attack or withdraw. You will feel as if you are on an emotional roller coaster. It is at this time, more than at any other, that you must regain control of yourself, your feelings, and your actions.

Psychologists have developed what is called the "locus of control" theory. According to this theory, each person has either an internal or an external locus of control, or something in between. It varies from person to person. An *internal* locus of control means you feel that you are in charge of your life and in command of the situation. As a result, you feel more calm, clear, and positive when things go wrong.

People with an *external* locus of control feel that they are largely controlled by people, circumstances, and events outside of themselves. They feel "out of control" and as a result, experience stress, negativity, and often psychosomatic illnesses.

SIX STAGES OF REGAINING CONTROL

Psychologist Elisabeth Kubler-Ross identified several stages a person goes through when grieving the death of a loved one, especially a spouse or child. But people also go through several similar stages when they experience an unexpected setback or reversal in their work or personal life.

1. *The first of these stages is denial.* "I don't believe it! This can't be happening!" is a common reaction in this stage. Denial—the refusal to face the inevitable and unavoidable reality of the situation—causes much mental anguish and unhappiness.

2. *The second stage of dealing with a death or setback is anger.* Once it is clear that the event has occurred, the person reacts with anger toward the person or situation he considers responsible for what has happened.

3. *Closely following anger is the third stage, blame.* The individual who has suffered a traumatic event or a loss of some kind immediately blames someone or something else for what has happened. His conversation with himself and others becomes an explanation of why and how he is innocent and why and how someone else is to blame for his unhappiness.

It is hardly possible for someone in a state of denial, anger, or blame to deal calmly and rationally with a situation or to move forward. These negative emotions are paralyzing and can keep you locked in place, as though your feet were in a bucket of hardened cement. No progress is possible.

4. *Once you have gone through denial, anger, and blame, the next stage in dealing with death or traumatic events is guilt.* You begin to feel that you did or failed to do something that led to or contributed to the problem. Feelings of guilt soon turn into feelings of negativity, inferiority, and depression. You may feel like giving up or feel sorry for yourself. It becomes easy to slip into self-pity and self-reproach.

5. *The true antidote to denial, anger, and blame is accepting responsibility.* It is only when you accept responsibility for your situation and for the way you respond to what has happened to you that you can deal with the problem and take control of the situation.

There is a direct relationship between the acceptance of responsibility and a sense of control. Furthermore, there is a direct relationship between a sense of control and positive emotions. The more that you accept responsibility for yourself and your situation, the greater sense of control you will have and the happier and more positive you will become.

What amazed me many years ago in my studies was the discovery of the power of those simple words: "I am responsible!" It is impossible to remain angry or to blame other people for problems in your life when you are saying, "I am responsible." The more you repeat the words "I am responsible" to yourself, the more you short-circuit or switch off the negative emotions that are clouding your judgment and making you unhappy.

At this point, you may feel like arguing by pointing out all the things that the other person or persons did to hurt you and why you are completely justified in feeling angry toward them. But it's important to remember an excellent question psychologist Jerald Jampolsky once asked: "Do you want to be right or do you want to be happy?"

In almost any negative situation or reversal in your personal or business life, you are at least partially responsible. Sometimes you are totally responsible, which will make you angrier than in any other situation. You did or failed to do certain things that led to the unexpected and undesirable event. You failed to do certain things or to make note of certain signs that indicated that something was wrong. In fact, the more responsible you realize you were for what happened, the greater will be your tendency initially to lash out and blame other people for your situation.

But this will not do. Accepting responsibility is a purely selfish act. You accept responsibility for one reason: to enable you to regain a sense of calmness, clarity, and personal control. Instead of feeling angry, unhappy, and frustrated, you accept responsibility and immediately feel calm and relaxed.

There are certainly situations when you are completely innocent, when what happened had nothing to do with you at all. As in a drive-by shooting, you were the victim of circumstances over which you had no control. But you are still responsible for your responses. Remember, it is not what happens to you, but how you *respond* to what happens to you that determines whether you are happy or unhappy. As Shakespeare wrote, "There is nothing either good or bad, but thinking makes it so."

6. *One of the most powerful tools that you can use to regain control of your mind is called reframing.* The way you feel about any situation is largely determined by your explanatory style—by how you interpret the event to yourself, in either a positive or negative way.

In reframing, you interpret the event in a positive way. You change your language. Instead of defining it as a problem, you reframe it as a situation. A problem is something that is upsetting and stressful. A situation is something that you simply deal with.

Better yet, you can reframe a situation as a challenge. A challenge is something that you rise to, that brings out the very best in you. A challenge is a positive experience that you look forward to.

Best of all, you can interpret an unexpected setback as an opportunity. Whereas a problem is something that sets you back and costs you time, money, and emotion, an opportunity is something that you move quickly to take advantage of.

Do you remember when I said that 299 out of 300 people who had accomplished great things with their lives attributed their success to unexpectedly losing a job? Rather than feeling denial, blame, or anger toward the boss or company who had laid them off or fired them, they saw their new freedom as a challenge and as an opportunity to reinvent themselves and do something completely different with their lives.

7. *Resurgence.* Once you have accepted responsibility, reinterpreted the negative event in a positive way, and taken complete control of your mind and emotions, you are ready to resume your upward journey. As Napoleon Hill said, "The only real cure for worry is purposeful action toward a predetermined goal."

You accept what has happened as inevitable and irreversible. You refuse to waste a minute worrying about the past or something that cannot be changed. Instead, you focus on the future, on the almost unlimited number of possibilities and opportunities open to you to create a wonderful life for yourself.

QUESTIONS FOR REFLECTION

1. In what one specific area of your life should you take some time to completely reevaluate your situation based on the reality of today?

2. How could you reorganize your life or work so that it is more in harmony with what you want and what makes you happy?

3. How could you restructure your life or work so that you are spending more time doing the things that bring you the greatest rewards?

4. How could you simplify your life by delegating, downsizing, consolidating, or eliminating low-value or no-value tasks and activities?

5. If you could wave a magic wand and reinvent your life completely, what changes would you make?

6. In what areas of your life do you need to accept complete responsibility so that you can start moving forward?

7. What one action are you going to take immediately as the result of what you have learned in this chapter?

CHAPTER TWO

Who Are You?

*"*Man, know thyself.*"*
—GREEK PROVERB

SELF-KNOWLEDGE, or self-awareness, is the starting point and the basic requirement of self-acceptance and self-esteem. The more you know and understand yourself, who you are, and how and why you think and feel the way you do, the more capable you are of making better decisions in every area of your life.

Recent surveys of older people, and especially those who have passed the hundred-year mark, asked them what they would have done differently if they could live their lives over again. Their answers were quite consistent.

The first thing these older people said was that they would have taken more risks and tried more things. They

23

would not have played it safe so much, but would have ventured into new jobs, activities, and relationships. They would not have been so concerned with the possibility of failure or of the criticism of the people around them. They would have taken more chances.

The second most-common answer was that they would have worried less. Instead of being continually preoccupied with money matters, health, family situations, and work concerns, they would have been more relaxed and realized that many of their most pressing concerns eventually resolved themselves and were not important at all.

The third and most important common response of older people, looking back on their lives, was that they would have taken the time to stop and think more about what was really important to them. They would not have allowed themselves to become so busy and caught up in life for so many years that they never thought about what they really wanted. In looking back, they saw that almost everything they had done was a response or reaction to the demands of another person or situation. Other people's decisions and demands had largely shaped their lives.

CALL A TIME-OUT

The sad fact is that we often become so busy with our daily lives that we seldom take the time to stop the clock completely and just think quietly about who we really are inside and what we really want for ourselves.

In times of transition, when one phase of our life comes to an end, we often receive what is called "a gift of time." Very much like calling a time-out in a football game, we can call a time-out in our own lives to reevaluate our current situations and decide upon a different game plan for the future, based on what we now know. Many of history's greats agree with this idea of taking time to reflect. For example, Socrates said, "The unexamined life is not worth living." Henry Ford said, "Thinking is the hardest work there is; which is the probable reason why so few people engage in it." And Thomas Edison said, "There are a few people who think, a few more who think they think, and then there are the great majority, who would rather die than think."

Your life is usually so busy that if you don't stop, turn everything off, and get off by yourself on a regular basis, your life will keep on going with the force of inertia. After all, Sir Isaac Newton's law of inertia says that a body in motion tends to remain in motion unless acted upon by an outside force. Today, we say, "The more you do what you are doing, the more you will get what you've got."

If you do not take sufficient time to think about yourself, your past, present, and future, you will think poorly, make more mistakes, and often get into worse situations than you have before. Blaise Pascal, the French author, wrote, "I have often said that man's unhappiness arises from one thing alone: that he cannot remain quietly in his room."

If you don't take the time to think, to analyze your life and your situation, you will often make hasty decisions that lead to unhappy outcomes. The rule is that people decisions, job decisions, and financial decisions made quickly are usually wrong decisions.

GIVE YOURSELF A COMPLETE EXAMINATION

In reinventing yourself, the best ideas about what to do and how to do it will usually come from taking the time to examine your past and present—the ideas and experiences that got you to where you are today. This is very much like getting a complete medical examination where the doctor orders a blood workup to analyze every chemical in your system. In this way, the doctor can identify deficiencies and make recommendations for improvements.

Knowledge, information, and experience only become relevant and valuable when someone asks a *question* about them. When you ask and answer focused questions about yourself and about how you really think and feel inside, you take a multidimensional snapshot from all sides that gives you a clear picture of the person you have become.

Here are some questions that will enable you to analyze yourself, understand who you really are, and understand what you want at a deeper level. Write your answers as quickly as you can. The less time you take to analyze and the more spontaneous you are, the more accurate your answers will be.

1. Each person lives from the inside out. Happy people are those who are very clear about what they believe in and what they stand for. Your true values are always expressed in your actions and behaviors. By the law of correspondence, your outer world will tend to be a mirror image of

the person you are inside. Clarity regarding your true values is essential. What are your three most important *values* in life, right now?

1. _____

2. _____

3. _____

2. What are the three *things* in life that are most important to you? The answer to this question will always be the three things—people, activities, and ideas—that trigger the strongest emotions in you when you think about them or talk about them. What are they?

1. _____

2. _____

3. _____

3. Your best qualities have taken you many years to develop. They are essential elements of your character. What are your three best *qualities* as a person?

1. _____

2. _____

3. _____

4. What three personal *accomplishments* in your life are you most proud of? Your answer to this question will tell a lot about yourself and will be a good indicator of your real values and what is truly important to you.

1. _____

2. _____

3. _____

5. What three skills or *abilities* are you the best at? These are usually the main reasons that you have been successful in your job or career. What are they?

1. _____

2. _____

3. _____

6. The "Law of Three" says that if you analyze a list of everything that you do in your work, you will find that three activities account for fully 90 percent of the contribution you make to yourself and your company. Much of your material success in life comes as a result of doing these three things more and becoming better at them. What are the three things that you do in your work that account for most of the contribution you make?

1. _____

2. _____

3. _____

7. In your work life, you have had "peak experiences" where you have accomplished something noteworthy. In most cases, these achievements were the result of hard work, persistence, and the application of your very best talents and abilities to the accomplishment of a specific result. What have been your three biggest *successes* in your career?

1. _____

2. _____

3. _____

8. You have special talents, abilities, and temperament that make you different from anyone else who has ever lived. It is when you use all three of these together in a task or job that you get the most pleasure from your work and achieve the best results. What are the three best *jobs*, or parts of jobs, you have ever had?

1. _____

2. _____

3. _____

9. What three job *activities* give you the greatest satisfaction? These are probably the activities that enable you to contribute the very most to your work and your company. Whatever gives you the greatest feeling of self-esteem is a good indicator of what you should be doing more of.

1. _____

2. _____

3. _____

10. If you were forced to take an extended period of time off from work and you had the money to do anything you wanted, how would you *spend the time*? Where would you go and what would you do?

1. _____

2. _____

3. _____

Your answer to this question is a good indication of what you should be doing more of in the future.

11. What are the three *worst* experiences you've had in your personal or business life?

1. _____

2. _____

3. _____

The answer to this question will be your most stressful and frustrating experiences, causing you major losses in time, money, and ego. But these three negative experiences have probably been some of the greatest learning opportunities of your life as well.

12. What are the three biggest mistakes you've made in your life?

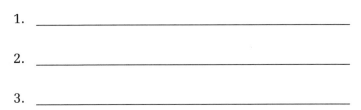

1. _____

2. _____

3. _____

These mistakes will almost invariably be decisions you made or failed to make as the result of fear or ignorance. Very often, if you are not careful, they will be major sources of regret that can hold you back from doing or trying new things in the future.

13. It seems that every lesson you learn is accompanied by pain of some kind—physical, mental, emotional, or financial. The mark of top people is that they look into every problem or difficulty for the lessons it might contain. Sometimes, these lessons become the stepping stones to greater success later in life. What are the three most important *lessons* you've learned in your life or career?

1. _____

2. _____

3. _____

14. What are your three biggest *worries* or concerns right now?

    1. _____

    2. _____

    3. _____

The greater clarity you have in answering this question, the more capable you are of taking action to resolve these worries or problems. Many people are unhappy, insecure, and distracted because they are not clear about the situations in their lives that are causing them stress or distress.

15. Who are the three people, living or dead, whom you most *admire*?

    1. _____

    2. _____

    3. _____

You always tend to admire or even love people whom you feel have values, virtues, and qualities that you most aspire to and would like to have in yourself. The answer to this question often tells you more about your deepest values and the qualities you would like to develop.

16. Who are three (or more) *people* you care about the most?

1. _____

2. _____

3. _____

The answers to this question will help you to remain focused on what is truly important to you—the key people in your life. Throughout your life, and especially in times of transition, you often take these people for granted. As a result, you do not give them the attention and treat them with the affection, respect, and courtesy that you should. Who are they?

17. What *qualities* in other people do you most admire?

1. _____

2. _____

3. _____

The qualities that you most admire in others are usually the qualities that you most aspire to have yourself. The greater clarity you have about these qualities, the easier it is for you to practice them whenever they are called for.

18. What *three words* would you like people to use to describe you to other people when you are not present?

1. _____

2. _____

3. _____

This is another values question. The best people are very thoughtful about how they want to be thought of and described by others. As a result, they consciously monitor their words and behaviors to ensure that the impression they make on others is consistent with the way they want to be talked about. This clarity of personal vision enables a person to shape and develop his or her own character and personality to an ever-higher level.

CONGRATULATIONS! Most people will never ask or answer these questions in their entire lives. Your answers help you to think better and more constructively about your past and present, and begin to give you insights into your future, which we will focus on in Chapter 3.

The historian George Santayana wrote, "Those who do not learn from history are doomed to repeat it." By looking deeply into yourself, and by becoming a more thoughtful and aware person, you can reinvent yourself in a positive and constructive way throughout your life.

QUESTIONS FOR REFLECTION

1. Think back: What have been the happiest moments of your life?

2. What do you most enjoy doing in your spare time?

3. What advice would you give your child or close friend who wanted to be successful in your field?

4. What is your best talent or skill; what are you really excellent at doing?

5. What one quality would you most like to develop in yourself?

6. What is the most important business lesson you have ever learned?

7. What is the most important personal lesson you have ever learned?

CHAPTER THREE

What Do You Want?

"If you don't know where you're going, any road will get you there."

—YOGI BERRA

WHEN I WAS 20 YEARS OLD, I set off to see the world. I had not graduated from high school and I had no marketable skills. The only jobs I could do were laboring jobs—washing dishes, working in sawmills and factories, living on farms and ranches, and working in construction, among others.

I worked my way across the country from the West Coast to the East Coast, got a job on a Norwegian freighter to cross the North Atlantic, and arrived in London at the age of 21. From there, I rode a bicycle across France and Spain to Gibraltar, pooled my money with two friends to buy a Land

Rover, and then drove across the Sahara Desert and south through Africa, finally arriving sick and exhausted in Johannesburg, South Africa, in 1965.

After this trip, I began asking the question, "Why are some people more successful than others?" This question, and my search for the answer, changed my life. From that moment on, I read every book I could find on success, listened to audio programs, attended seminars, and immersed myself in the subject. Very soon, I found that the primary reason some people were more successful than others was quite simple: They thought differently, made different decisions, took different actions, and got different results. This insight opened my eyes forever.

THE ANSWERS HAVE BEEN FOUND

When I got into sales, after struggling for many months, I began asking, "Why are some salespeople more successful than others?" I began asking for advice from the top salespeople, and they gave it to me generously. I started doing what they told me to do, and my sales went up. Soon, my sales were so high that I was invited to become a sales manager.

I then began asking, "Why are some sales managers more successful than others?" I went to the other sales managers in my industry and asked them for advice, which they gave me. I then did what they told me to do, and within a year, I had recruited, trained, and fielded 95 salespeople. I went from rags to riches. My life changed completely.

What I discovered, in retrospect, was the law of cause and effect. This law says that there is a cause for every effect. If you can be clear about the effect that you want, you can then trace it back to someone who at sometime did not have what you want but has now acquired it, and if you do the same things that he or she did, you will soon get the same results.

THE IRON LAW

The law of cause and effect is also called the iron law of the universe. It was first taught by Aristotle in about 350 B.C. and called at that time the Aristotelian Principle of Causality. This principle went on to become a basic tenet of Western civilization.

The law of cause and effect is the basis of the scientific method. All other laws and principles in the fields of mathematics, science, medicine, mechanics, technology, aeronautics, and economics all fall under the law of cause and effect and are subsets of this law.

In the Bible, the law is called the law of sowing and reaping. This version says that, "Whatsoever a man soweth, that shall he also reap." In other words, what you put in, you get out. Sir Isaac Newton called the idea the law of action and reaction; that is, for every action there is an equal and opposite reaction. Ralph Waldo Emerson called it the law of compensation. He said that for whatever you do in life, you will be compensated in equal measure sooner or later.

What this law means for you is simple. If you can be absolutely clear about something that you want, you can then find other people who have already achieved it. If you do the same things that they did, over and over again, you will eventually get the same results.

The flip side of this principle is simple as well. If you do not do what other successful people do, over and over, you will not get the results that they get.

THE POWER OF THOUGHT

If you do what other successful people do, in any field, you eventually get the same results they do. There are virtually no limits.

Perhaps the most important application of this law, which is one of the foundation principles of all religion, philosophy, metaphysics, psychology, and success, is this: "Thoughts are causes, and conditions are effects."

Your thoughts are creative. Whatever you think about emotionally, positive or negative, creates a force field of energy that moves you toward your goals and moves your goals toward you.

THE LAW OF BELIEF

The law of belief, a subset of this principle, says that whatever you believe with conviction becomes your reality.

Nineteenth-century Harvard psychology professor William James said, "Belief creates the actual fact."

If you believe that you are destined to live a wonderful life and be happy, healthy, thin, and prosperous, and you hold to that belief long enough and hard enough, it will eventually become your reality.

Your beliefs act like a program in your mental computer. They direct and guide you to do more of the things that make your beliefs come true and avoid doing those things that might hold you back.

And how can you tell what your true beliefs are? Simple. Look at your behavior. It is not what you say, or wish, or hope, or intend that indicates what you truly believe, but only what you do moment to moment, especially when you are under pressure of some kind.

When you are put under severe strain or have a setback, difficulty, or emergency, your true beliefs emerge in your behavior. As Epictetus, the Greek philosopher, wrote, "Circumstances do not make the man; they merely reveal him to himself" (and to others, as well).

THE LAW OF EXPECTATIONS

The law of expectations says that "whatever you expect, with confidence, becomes your own self-fulfilling prophecy." In other words, your innermost beliefs and convictions shape your expectations and cause you to approach the world in a manner consistent with them.

If you expect to be successful, happy, prosperous, and popular, you will act in a way consistent with these expectations and they will become your self-fulfilling prophesies.

You are always telling your own fortune by the way you think and talk about the way things are going to work out for you. Successful people develop an attitude of "positive expectations" no matter what is happening around them. As a result, they are more positive and effective in everything they do. They make more money, are happier with their lifestyles, and are more popular than people with negative attitudes and beliefs.

THE LAW OF ATTRACTION

The law of attraction says that you are a living magnet. You invariably attract into your life the people, circumstances, and resources that are in harmony with your dominant thoughts, especially those thoughts magnetized by the power of emotion, either positive or negative.

One of the great dangers of experiencing a sudden reversal or unexpected transition in your life is that you can very easily interpret the experience in a negative way. When you do this, quite innocently, you set up a force field of negative energy that attracts even more negative experiences into your life. This is the meaning of the saying "When it rains, it pours."

These principles have been taught for more than 5,000 years and are the foundations of the thinking of many of the greatest men and women in history.

THE BOTTOM LINE

The bottom line of these laws and principles is this: You become what you think about most of the time. This is an astonishing idea for most people, especially people whose general tone of thinking is negative or critical. People don't want to believe that their own mental attitudes are largely responsible for most of the problems in their lives.

The good news is that the only thing in the world that you can control is your own thinking. When you discipline yourself to keep your thinking focused on what you want and off of the things that you don't want, you remain positive, optimistic, and in control of your life. When you ask successful, happy people about their habitual ways of thinking, you find that they are almost always thinking about what they want and how to get it.

By the law of substitution, which says that you can substitute one thought for another, when you think about what you want and how to get it, you immediately become positive and focused, and all negativity disappears. You think with greater clarity, make better decisions, and take more effective actions. You get better results. The achievement of positive results triggers the release of endorphins in your brain, nature's "happy drug."

The more positive and happy you feel about your accomplishments, the more endorphins are released and the happier and more positive you become. This then motivates you to do even more positive and constructive things, which gives you even better results, which repeats the positive process over again. That's why people say "Nothing succeeds like success."

LOOK WHERE YOU ARE GOING

Successful people are intensely future-oriented. They think about the future most of the time. They think about where they are going rather than where they have been. They think about what they want and how to get it.

Future-orientation is the mark of the leader, in any area. As management guru Peter Drucker said, "The responsibility of the leader is to think about the future; no one else can." Michael Kami, a well-known strategic planner, says, "Those who do not think about the future cannot have one." Author and management expert Alec Mackenzie agrees, saying, "The best way to predict the future is to create it."

Future-oriented people practice a special behavior called idealization. When you practice idealization, you project forward and imagine that your future is perfect in every way. You create an exciting vision of the kind of life you want to live and the kind of person you want to be.

YOUR FIVE-YEAR FANTASY

When I do strategic planning for corporations, I begin by asking the executives in attendance to describe what this company would look like in five years if it were the very best in that industry. I go around the room and ask for a contribution from each person, which I then write on flip charts and post on the wall. When I have exhausted all the positive, descriptive words and phrases regarding product quality, customer service, leadership, reputation, financial strength, growth rates, respect for individuals, and others, I then revisit the list.

I ask lots of questions. Which of these descriptions are causes and which are effects? What are inputs and what are outputs? What do we need to accomplish before we accomplish something else? We then organize the list of attractive features in order of priority with a clear description of this company as if it were perfect sometime in the future. I then ask the executives this key question: "Is this possible?"

One by one, each of the executives begins to nod and say, "Yes, these are all possible. Maybe not in one year, but they can definitely be accomplished within five years, if we commit to achieving them." For the rest of the strategic-planning session, often taking two or three days, we discuss and agree on the specific steps that we can take, starting today, to create the ideal corporation of the future in that industry.

BACK-FROM-THE-FUTURE THINKING

You can do this same exercise in your own life. Begin by imagining that you have no limitations at all. Imagine for a moment that you have everything you need: all the time and all the money, all the education and all the experience, all the friends and all the contacts, and that you could be, have, or do anything you wanted in the whole world in the most important areas in your life.

Create a "five-year fantasy" and practice "back from the future" thinking. Project yourself forward five years and imagine your life is ideal in every way at that time. What would it look like? What would you be doing? What would you no longer be doing? What would you have, for yourself and your family? If your life were perfect in every way, how would it be different from today?

From this vantage point in the future, in your own mind, look back to where you are today and imagine the steps that you would need to take to get from where you are to where you want to be. Especially, determine the first step. Then, have the courage to step out in faith in the direction of your dreams. The willingness and the courage to take the first step is often the turning point in your life.

SEVEN MAIN AREAS OF LIFE

There are seven main areas of life. Imagine you could wave a magic wand and make your life perfect in each area. What would it look like?

1. Business and Career

If your business, your career, and your company were perfect five years from today, what would they look like? How would they be different from today? How much would you be earning? What would you be doing? With whom would you be working? What would be your level of authority and responsibility? How would you be spending your time, day in and day out? If your work life were perfect, what would it look like?

1. _____

2. _____

3. _____

2. Family and Relationships

If your family life were perfect in every way, what would it look like? How would it be different from today? What kind of a lifestyle would you be living? What kind of a home would you live in? What sort of things would you want to do for and with your family? What sort of vacations would you take? Most of all, how would you feel in your relationships with the most important people in your life if your family life were perfect in every way?

1. _____

2. _____

3. _____

3. Health and Fitness

If your health were perfect sometime in the future, how would it be different from today? How much would you weigh? How fit would you be? What kind of energy levels would you have? What would you be doing differently with regard to diet and exercise? What changes would you have to make in your health regimen today for you to have superb health and fitness sometime in the future?

1. _____

2. _____

3. _____

4. Financial Independence

If you were financially independent, how much would you have in the bank? How much money would you have invested? Most of all, how much passive income would you be receiving each month and each year from your accumulated savings and investments? What is the amount that you will have to have working for you so that you can retire on a comfortable income and never have to worry about money again? What steps could you take, starting today, to accumulate this amount?

1. _____

2. _____

3. _____

5. Knowledge and Skill

What additional knowledge and skill will you need to be able to earn the kind of money that you want to earn, so that you can enjoy the kind of lifestyle that you want to enjoy? Remember, whatever got you to where you are today will not get you any further. To become someone you have never been before, you must learn and practice skills that you have never had before. What are they?

1. _____

2. _____

3. _____

6. Social and Community Involvement

If you could wave a magic wand, what would you like to be doing in your country or community? What causes would you like to support or work for? What would you like to achieve?

1. _____

2. _____

3. _____

7. Spiritual Development and Inner Peace

If your life were perfect, how would you spend your time to achieve ever-higher levels of inner growth and peace of mind? Think of the times in your life when you have been the happiest and felt the greatest sense of inner peace. What could you do to duplicate and increase those moments?

1. _____

2. _____

3. _____

CONGRATULATIONS! Most people have never asked and answered these questions in their lives. You now know more about yourself and what is really important to you than perhaps ever before.

THREE ENEMIES TO AVOID

When you think about these questions and answers, there are three enemies that may emerge to sabotage your hopes and dreams. These have been the three greatest enemies of mankind from time immemorial.

The first enemy is the comfort zone. This is the natural tendency of most people to become comfortable and complacent in their current work or lifestyles, and to resist changing in any way. But change is the law of growth, and growth is the law of life. If you don't move out of your comfort zone, you cannot make any progress. Remember, the more you do what you are doing, the more you will get of what you've got.

You must continually force yourself to move out of your comfort zone into your discomfort zone. There is no other way to change or improve your life in any way. The trap of the comfort zone is one of the greatest of all enemies of success and progress.

The second enemy you must face is called learned helplessness. Learned helplessness is triggered by the fear of failure or by the fear of loss of some kind. The fear of failure is the major reason for failure in adult life. It is expressed in the words *I can't.*

Whenever you think of something new, different, risky, or uncertain, you may immediately think of all the reasons why it's not possible. You may think that you don't have the resources or the ability. You may feel that you don't have the money or the contacts. You will think of the possibility of loss of time, money, or emotion. The fear of failure makes you freeze inside, like a deer caught in the headlights, and triggers the reaction of learned helplessness.

The way you get out of your comfort zone and overcome your fears of failure and helplessness is by setting big goals and then by throwing your whole heart into their accomplishment. Your ability to set goals and make plans for their success is the true master skill of success.

The third enemy of success is the natural tendency to follow the path of least resistance, to continually seek for fast, easy, enjoyable ways to do things. Following this path leads to searching for get-rich-quick methods and easy money.

Anything worthwhile takes a long period of hard work and single-minded concentration to achieve. You must resist the siren song of the path of least resistance and discipline yourself to do what is hard and necessary to achieve the goals that are truly possible for you.

THE QUICK-LIST METHOD

As quickly as you can, in 30 seconds or less for each question, write down your answers to the following.

1. What are your three most important *business and career* goals, right now?

    1. _____

    2. _____

    3. _____

2. What are your three most important *family and relationship* goals, right now?

    1. _____

    2. _____

    3. _____

3. What are your three most important *health and fitness* goals, right now?

    1. _____

    2. _____

    3. _____

4. What are your three most important *financial* goals right now?

    1. _____

    2. _____

    3. _____

5. What are your three most important *educational* or learning goals right now?

    1. _____

    2. _____

    3. _____

6. What are your three most important *social and community* goals right now?

    1. _____

    2. _____

    3. _____

7. What are your three most important goals for *spiritual development and inner peace* right now?

1. _____

2. _____

3. _____

WHEN YOU ONLY HAVE 30 seconds to write down the answers to these questions, your answers will be as accurate as if you had 30 minutes or three hours.

Once you have written down your answers, you should sit down and share them with your spouse or another important person in your life. If you are married, have the other person answer these questions privately, and then compare your answers. You will often be surprised at what each of you has written.

THE MASTER SKILL OF SUCCESS

In a famous study in 1953, often refuted, the graduating seniors of a major university were asked if they had written goals, and plans to achieve them, after they left the university.

It turned out that 3 percent had written goals and plans. Fourteen percent had goals but they were not written. The other 83 percent had no goals or plans at all, aside from getting out of the university and going on vacation that summer.

Twenty years later, in 1973, they followed up on the graduates in this study and asked them, among other things, about their financial situations. They found that the 3 percent of students who had clear, written goals and plans upon graduation were worth more than the entire other 97 percent of graduates put together.

GOALS, PLANS, AND INCOME

Not to be outdone, another major university that had heard about this survey asked students graduating from its own business school in 1979 the same question: Do you have written goals and plans for your future when you leave this university?

Again, the results were identical. Three percent of the graduating seniors had clear, written goals and plans. Fourteen percent had goals, but they were not in writing. The other 83 percent had no clear goals at all.

Ten years later, in 1989, it followed up on these students to find out how well they had done in the previous decade. They found that those students who had goals that were not written down were earning on average twice as much as the 83 percent of students who left college with no goals at all. But to their surprise, they found that the 3 percent of students who started off with clear, written goals and plans were earning on average ten times as much as the other 97 percent put together.

DRIVING ACROSS COUNTRY

Here is an example that demonstrates the importance of goals. Imagine that you have two drivers, each with a brand new Mercedes-Benz. They both set out to travel across the country toward a distant destination. But one of them, in his haste to get going, sets off with no road map and on roads where there are no road signs.

The second driver takes the time to plan his trip carefully, using a road map and getting advice about the road ahead. He is thoroughly supplied with food, gasoline, and water. He takes a little bit more time before starting out, but when he starts out he is thoroughly prepared.

Which of these two drivers is most likely to reach his destination on schedule? The answer is obvious. The first driver will drive north and south, and east and west, and often go around in circles, using up all his gasoline and making no progress at all. The second driver will drive straight and true, like an arrow flying through the air, toward his clearly defined destination following his road map every step of the way.

Life is very much the same. People with clear, specific goals and plans that they work from each day, accomplish, on average, ten times as much as other people with equal education and abilities, but who have no clear idea of where they are going or when they want to get there.

GOAL-SETTING MADE SIMPLE

Here is a powerful goal-setting formula that you can use to accomplish any goal that you can set for yourself.

Step One: Decide *exactly* what you want and write it down in the present tense. Be specific. Your goal should be so clear that a child could read it and explain it clearly to another child.

1. _____

2. _____

3. _____

Step Two: Set a *deadline* for the achievement of your goal. Because of the fear of failure, many people set vague or unrealistic goals and avoid committing themselves to a timeline. As a result, they have no benchmarks or standards to measure their progress, and they eventually give up and quit.

1. _____

2. _____

3. _____

Step Three: Determine the *obstacles* that you will have to overcome to achieve your goal. Identify the major constraints that hold you back from achieving your goal at the present time. Fully 80 percent of the reasons you are not achieving the goals are *internal*. They result from your lack of some quality or ability, which is largely under your control. Only 20 percent of the obstacles or difficulties that are holding you back are external, in other people or situations.

1. _____

2. _____

3. _____

Step Four: Identify the additional *knowledge and skills* that you will need to achieve your goal. The fact is that you have gone about as far as you can go in life with the skills you have now. To go any further, you are going to have to improve in certain areas and develop additional skills.

1. _____

2. _____

3. _____

Step Five: Identify the people, groups, and organizations whose *cooperation* you will require to achieve your goals. Include your boss, your customers, your family, your friends, and your sources of finance.

1. _____

2. _____

3. _____

Step Six: Make a *plan* out of your answers to the previous questions. A plan is a list of activities organized by sequence and priority. A list organized by sequence means that you decide what you must do before you do something else. When you organize your list by priority, you determine what is more important on your list and what is less important. What should you do first, and what is most important? Write your list in order of priority.

1. _____

2. _____

3. _____

4. _____

5. _____

Once you have organized your list, you have the winning combination of a goal and a plan. With a goal and a plan, you will accomplish extraordinary things, and far faster than you can imagine today.

Step Seven: Take *action* on your plan immediately. Step out in faith. Once you begin, do something every day that moves you in the direction of your most important goal, whatever it is at that time. What one action are you going to take immediately?

_____

_____

_____

GOAL-SETTING EXERCISE

Here is a goal-setting exercise that can change your life: Make a list of ten goals that you would like to accomplish in the next year or so. Write them in the present tense as though you had already achieved them. Start each goal with the word *I*. You are the only person in the universe who can use the word *I* in reference to yourself. Follow the word *I* with an action verb of some kind: "I earn," "I weigh," "I achieve," "I drive," or "I acquire."

When you precede a goal statement with the word *I* plus an action verb, it is like pushing down on the plunger of a dynamite detonator. This command activates your subconscious and superconscious minds, triggering ideas and energy that begin to move you toward your goal, and your goal toward you.

1. _____

2. _____

3. _____

4. _____

5. _____

6. _____

7. _____

8. _____

9. _____

10. _____

Once you have completed your list, review your list and imagine that you have a magic wand. Imagine that you could have all of these goals sooner or later if you wanted them long enough and hard enough, but you could have one goal within 24 hours.

Which one goal, if you achieved it immediately, would have the greatest positive impact on your life? Which one goal would help you to achieve more of your other goals? Which one goal would bring you the greatest happiness and satisfaction if you could accomplish it immediately?

Whatever your answer to that question, put a circle around that goal. This goal then becomes your "Major Definite Purpose" in life. This goal becomes the central organizing principle of your life and activities. This becomes the goal that you think about most of the time.

TAKING ACTION

Take a clean sheet of paper and write this goal down in the present tense.

Set a deadline. Make the goal measurable.

Determine the obstacles and difficulties you will have to overcome to achieve this goal.

Determine the knowledge and skills that you will need.

Determine the people, groups, and organizations whose cooperation you will require to achieve this goal.

Make a list of all of your answers and organize them by sequence and priority.

Finally, take action immediately on your plan. When you get up in the morning, think about your goal. All day long, think about your goal. At the end of the day, review your progress toward your goal.

UNLOCK YOUR MENTAL POWERS

As you think about your goal more, you activate all your mental powers. By the law of cause and effect, your thoughts about your goal are the causes, and the achievement of your goal will be the effect.

By the law of belief, the more you believe that you will achieve this goal, the more things you will do to attain it, and the faster it becomes your reality. By the law of expectations, the more you expect your goal to materialize in your life, the more things you will do to make it come true. By the law of attraction, the more you think about your goal—with confidence and enthusiasm—the more you will magnetize your mind and attract into your life the people and resources you need to achieve your goal.

SELF-DIRECTION AND PERSONAL POWER

In times of transition, when you are reinventing yourself, your ability to set clear goals for your future and then to work toward the achievement of those goals every day increases your self-esteem, self-respect, and personal pride. It fills you with a sense of forward motion and accomplishment. It gives you a feeling of personal power.

When you develop absolute clarity about your goals and work on them everyday, you take complete control of your life in every area.

QUESTIONS FOR REFLECTION

1. What one goal would you most like to attain in your job, career, or business?

2. What one goal would you most like to achieve in your family and your relationships?

3. What one health and fitness goal would you like to achieve?

4. What one financial goal would you like to achieve?

5. What one subject or skill would you like to master?

6. What one contribution would you like to make to your country or community?

7. What one thing would you like to do to increase your peace of mind?

CHAPTER FOUR

What Are You Worth?

"Our destiny changes with our thought; we shall become what we wish to become, do what we wish to do, when our habitual thought corresponds with our desires."

—ORISON SWETT MARDEN, FOUNDER OF *SUCCESS* MAGAZINE

SOMETIMES I WILL STOP in the middle of a seminar and ask the audience this question: "Who is the most important person in this room?"

This question is usually greeted with silence. After a few moments, someone will say "You," or "Me," or "The boss"; at this point I acknowledge the person who said "Me" and confirm his statement by saying, "You're right." I then refer to everyone in the audience and say, "You are each the most important person in this room. You are the most important person in your entire world. Your entire world revolves around you as an individual."

Psychologists tell us that how important you feel you are—that is, how much you like and respect yourself—is the critical determinant of the quality of your life. The more you like and respect yourself, the more you like and respect others, and the more they like and respect you in return.

When you genuinely like yourself, you set bigger goals for yourself, and you persist longer to achieve them. When you feel valuable and important, you take better care of yourself in every way. The more you like yourself, the more self-confidence you have, the more risks you are willing to take, and the more new things you are willing to try.

THE PURSUIT OF HAPPINESS

The United States is remarkable in history because it was the first country to draw up a declaration of independence and a written constitution that put the individual at the center of all political activity. The Declaration of Independence says, "We hold these truths to be self-evident, that all men are created equal, that they are endowed by their Creator with certain unalienable Rights, that among these are Life, Liberty, and the pursuit of Happiness."

As an individual, as a matter of fact and of law, you are extremely valuable and important. You are important to your parents, who brought you into the world. You are important to your spouse and your children. You are important to your friends and your society. You are important to your customers and your co-workers. Simply because you are alive, you have inherent worth, value, dignity, pride, and entitlement to the respect of others. In our democratic society, our political system revolves around you, the individual voter. Your vote has exactly the same power as a vote carried by the richest and most powerful person in the country.

YOUR LABOR IS A COMMODITY

In the workplace, however, the situation is completely different. As an employee at any level, you represent a unit of labor, a factor of production, a human commodity to be deployed and used to achieve the greatest benefit, advantage, or profit for your company and your customers.

Each person sees his personal work as something special, unique, and different, as an extension of her own personality and an essential part of his life. But we view the work, products, or services of others, as commodities that we try to obtain on the best possible terms.

As a producer, you seek the very most for the very least. As a consumer, however, when you go shopping, you constantly look for the highest quality at the lowest possible price. Your work and the value of what you do is looked upon by everyone else as merely a factor of production, something to be acquired at the lowest possible price in comparison with what else is available.

As an individual, you are an *economist* in your personal affairs. This means that you economize and try to get the very most output from the very least amount of input.

You attempt to sell your services at the highest possible price the market will pay.

DEFINITION OF A JOB

A job of any kind can be defined as a certain quality and quantity of a specific kind of work that can be combined with the work of other people to create a product or service that a customer, seeking the highest quality and lowest price, will buy.

In a market economy, customers pay all wages and salaries. The company is merely the middleman between the customer and the employee. Wages and salaries represent 60 percent to 80 percent of the costs of business operations in any field. When sales decline in any company, people often must be laid off if the company is going to survive. If you work for a government organization or a nonprofit, the unit of work you sell to your employer is combined with the work of others to accomplish a prescribed result.

As an individual, you are invaluable. There is no price that can be set on your personal life and physical well-being. But as an employee, and even a company owner, your value is determined solely by what people, customers, and employers are willing to pay for the work you do.

YOUR MOST VALUABLE ASSET

What is your most valuable financial asset? Whenever I ask this, people start thinking about their homes, cars, businesses, or personal investments.

The fact is that your ability to earn money, which has taken you all of your life to develop, is the most valuable thing you have. You could lose your job, your home, your car, and all of your savings through circumstances beyond your control. But as long as you can go back into the market and apply your earning ability to get results for which others will pay, you can draw tens of thousands of dollars into your life every year.

Most people take their earning ability for granted. They allow it to evolve and develop in a random and haphazard fashion. They get an education, most of which has little value in the workplace, and then they get their first jobs. They do what they are told to do and learn the essential skills necessary to do their jobs well enough so they don't get fired. Later, people come along and offer them other jobs, which they accept under the same conditions.

The careers of most people unfold accidently. They go from job to job and position to position, reacting and responding to what other people say and want. Because they do not look upon their ability to work and get results as a special resource, their careers are largely shaped by the decisions of others.

PERSONAL STRATEGIC PLANNING

In corporate strategic planning, companies restructure and reorganize assets, products, services, people, and money in order to increase return on equity (ROE). Equity is defined as total assets minus total liabilities. Return on equity is a key measure of management quality and of the efficiency with which the company is operated.

In personal strategic planning your entire focus in your work life is similar. It is to increase ROE as well. But in this case, ROE stands for return on energy. Sometimes we refer to this as "Return on Life."

Just as companies try to increase their return on financial capital, your job throughout your career is to increase your return on your human capital—mental, emotional, physical—invested in your career. Your job is to maximize your earning ability.

PRESIDENT OF YOUR OWN COMPANY

Sometimes, I ask my audiences, "How many people here are self-employed?" After waiting for a few seconds, people begin to raise their hands throughout the audience. On average about 10 percent to 15 percent of attendees raise their hands and acknowledge that they are self-employed.

Then I make this statement: "We are all self-employed."

From the time you take your first job until the time you retire, you are self-employed. You work for yourself, no matter who signs your paycheck. You are the president of "You, Inc.," an entrepreneurial company with one employee: yourself. Your company has one product to sell in a competitive market: your personal services.

The biggest mistake you can ever make is to think that you work for anyone else but yourself. You are always self-employed.

As the president of your own personal-services company, you are 100 percent responsible for your own personal strategic planning. You are responsible for every function of your business, even though it only consists of a single person with a single product. The skill and competence with which you carry out your personal business functions largely determines the course of your career, the quality of your life, and the height of your earning ability.

PLANNING FOR SUCCESS

There are six parts of the strategic planning process that apply to the management of your career:

1. *Marketing.* You are responsible for marketing and promoting yourself in a competitive market. You must continually improve the way you market yourself so that you can get the best job at the highest pay. As the saying goes, all strategic planning is market planning.

2. *Production.* You are responsible for producing the highest quantity of the most important and profitable products and services that your employer requires. You are responsible for results. Once you have marketed yourself well and gotten the ideal job, your entire future in your career will be determined by your ability to do your job well.

3. *Quality Control.* As the president of your own personal-services company, you are completely responsible for the quality of your work and for continually increasing that level of quality. High-quality work increases your earning ability; low-quality work decreases it.

4. *Training and Development.* As the head of your own company, you are completely responsible for your own training and development and for upgrading the skills and abilities of your staff—yourself.

You are responsible for reading books and magazines to help you do your work better. You are responsible for listening to CDs and watching DVDs to upgrade your skills. You are responsible for seeking out seminars and courses to stay abreast of trends in your field and learn new skills for the future.

5. *Finances.* You are responsible for all money coming into your personal company. You are responsible for your income and for what you do with that money.

6. *Organizational Development.* You are responsible for continually reorganizing and restructuring your personal business so that you are producing more products and services of a higher quality, in a more efficient manner.

According to one study, only 3 percent of employees see themselves as self-employed. Not surprisingly, these are the most respected people in any organization. They treat the company as though it belongs to them. They react personally to everything that happens to the company, either positive or negative. They come in a little earlier, work a little harder, and stay a little later. As a result, they are given more opportunities for learning and advancement. The company does everything possible to increase their earning ability and then pays them more for the increased value of their services.

SEVEN AREAS OF STRATEGIC THINKING

As the president of your own personal-services company, you are responsible for the seven areas of strategic thinking in the life of your business. The better you think and act in each of these areas, the more valuable you become, the more results you achieve, and the higher will be your earning ability.

1. *Specialization.* Each business must specialize to be successful. It must stand out in the market and be known by customers as one of the foremost companies in that industry.

A business can specialize in a particular product or service, a particular type of customer, or a particular type of market. Microsoft specializes in software. Wal-Mart specializes in people who live from paycheck to paycheck. A convenience store specializes in serving the local market.

In the same way, to maximize your earning ability, you must specialize as well. You may perform many functions in the course of your work life, but you must specialize in one or more jobs that are valuable or important to your employer.

2. *Differentiation.* Each company and each product or service must have a competitive advantage, an area of excellence, if it is going to survive in a competitive market. It must be superior to rival offerings in some clear, unmistakable and important way.

Because your sole product is you, you must differentiate yourself as well. You must be absolutely excellent in performing a specific function that is of great value to your employer. You must dedicate yourself to pay any price and work any number of hours to be the best in a particular area that is highly valued and pays well.

It is amazing how many people work away at their jobs for years, performing at the average or slightly above average level, when with a little extra work and skill they could be in the top 20 percent in their fields and earning the best money available for people in their fields.

3. *Segmentation.* In business, you seek out those customers in your niche who most desire your product or service and who most value your competitive advantage. You do not try to sell to everyone. You segment your markets so that you can sell to just those customers who are the most likely to buy your offerings and who will pay the most.

As an individual, you must segment as well. Many people transform their lives and their careers by going to work for companies that need the special talents and experience they developed in previous jobs. For example, Meg Whitman, the highly esteemed former president and CEO of eBay, was hired away from another job as eBay began to grow rapidly. Her unique combination of talents, skills, experience, and personality enabled her to transform eBay into one of the largest companies on the Internet, making her a billionaire in the process.

4. *Concentration.* In business, for a company to succeed, it must concentrate its limited promotional resources for marketing and advertising on just those customers who are the most likely to buy the product or service offered.

As an individual, you must concentrate single-mindedly as well on just those areas where excellent performance can bring about extraordinary results for yourself and your personal-services business.

5. *Positioning.* In business, a company must establish a perception in the minds and hearts of the customers it hopes to attract and keep. If one of your customers were to describe your company to a prospective customer, what words would he or she use? What words would be useful for them to use?

You must think about your personal positioning as well. Positioning refers to the words that come to a person's mind when he or she thinks about you. How would you like to be described by others when you are not there? Your choice of these words, and the way you coordinate your activities to ensure that people think of you with these words, can have an incredible impact on your work life.

6. *Branding.* In companies, branding refers to the value perception that people in the market have of a product or service. A brand has best been defined as the promises you make and the promises you keep. For example, people think of a Mercedes in terms of quality engineering. People think of FedEx in terms of getting something somewhere absolutely, positively overnight. People think about Apple as high quality and innovative. What is your personal brand? What promises do you make when people hire you and buy your services? What promises do you keep to your employer and your customers?

7. *Innovation.* For a company to survive in a fast-moving economy, it must be innovating continually and producing faster, better, cheaper products and services that are easier to use—before its competitors can. If you do not innovate continually, your competitors will, and they will soon pass you by. Once you have been passed by your competitors, it is very difficult to catch up.

You must be continually improving your service offerings as well. You must be continually seeking out faster, better, cheaper, more convenient ways to offer your services at a higher level of quality, in greater quantities, and at the same or lower prices to a demanding employer or customer market.

IN CHAPTER 1, I said that the most important work in America, or the world, is "thinking." Each of these concepts of personal strategic planning and strategic thinking are tools that you can use to think and plan more effectively, and make better decisions.

You could be weak in just one area. This weakness alone could undermine your earning ability and hold you back from realizing your full potential as a prized employee or money maker in a competitive market.

THE SEVEN ELEMENTS OF YOUR PERSONAL STRATEGIC PLAN

The greater clarity you have in each of these seven areas, the better decisions you will make and the more valuable your work will be.

1. Values

What are your personal and business values? What do you stand for and believe in? What principles would you not compromise, no matter what the temptation?

_____

_____

_____

In every company in which I have done strategic planning, the number-one value people choose is always integrity. The second values may be quality of products and services, caring about people, excellent customer service, profitability, innovation, entrepreneurship, and others. But integrity always comes first.

2. Vision

Based on your values, what is your vision for yourself and your career? If you had no limitations, what would your perfect job or career look like in the years ahead?

_____

_____

_____

3. Mission

Your mission is a statement of what you want to accomplish with your life and what kind of a person you want to be sometime in the future. A mission always includes a measure and a method.

Most mission statements are vague and rambling. They have no clarity of focus. It is not possible for even the sincerest person to become excited by them. An excellent mission statement gives you clarity and direction. It also gives a measure by which you know if your mission has been accomplished. Here's an example: "My mission is to be rated one of the top 10 percent of people in my field and as a result earn $150,000 per year by December 31, 2010." What is your mission?

_____

_____

_____

4. Purpose

Your purpose is defined as the reason you do what you do. Why do you get up in the morning? Why do you work as hard as you do? Your purpose is always defined in terms of the difference that you are making in the lives of other people. What is your purpose?

_____

_____

_____

5. Goals

Once you are clear about your values, vision, mission, and purpose, you then set clear, measurable goals or benchmarks that you need to achieve to be successful as an individual. You can have goals for personal income, income growth, bonuses, stock options, and results that you will need to attain in order to achieve your personal and financial objectives. What are your goals?

1. Personal income? _____

2. Income growth? _____

3. Bonuses? _____

4. Amount invested? _____

5. Annual passive income? _____

6. Priorities

The top 20 percent of your activities will be worth 80 percent of the value of everything you do. You apply the 80/20 Rule every single day to everything that you have to do. Always focus on those few things that you can do each day that can make the greatest and most valuable contribution to yourself and your life. What are your most valuable activities?

_____

_____

_____

7. Activities

These are the specific actions that you take every day, in harmony with your priorities and in alignment with your goals. There seems to be a direct relationship between activity and success. The more things you try, the more likely it is that you will triumph. What are your most important daily activities?

_____

_____

_____

WHEN YOU GO THROUGH a period of transition, especially entailing the loss of a job for any reason, it is essential that you take some time to stand back and evaluate your career.

Resist the temptation to rush back in and take a job identical to the one you just left. Remember, unexpectedly losing a job can be a wonderful opportunity to reinvent yourself more along the lines of what is really important to you in life.

INCREASE YOUR CONTRIBUTION

Perhaps the word that most determines your earning ability is *contribution*.

Your rewards will always be in direct proportion to the value of your service to others. Your income will be a direct reflection of the value of your contribution to your company. Throughout your career, you should be continually upgrading your skills and your ability to render ever-higher levels of service and contribution.

To increase your earning ability, you must increase the value of your contribution. Keep asking: "What can I do to increase the value of my service to my company today?" You must continually be looking for ways to put in more than you take out. Ultimately, your goal is to be "free" to your employer. For you to be "free" you must contribute so much value that even after the company has paid you generously it is well ahead for having you on the payroll.

There are no limits to how valuable you can make yourself in the months and years ahead. But you are in charge. You are responsible. You're the president of your own personal-services corporation. It's up to you.

QUESTIONS FOR REFLECTION

1. What is the most valuable thing you do, the most valuable skill you have?

2. What is your personal area of excellence, your competitive advantage?

3. What one great thing would you dare to dream if you knew that you could not fail?

4. If you had a $20,000,000 net worth and just learned that you only had 10 years left to live, what changes would you make in your life?

5. What have you always wanted to do in life but have been afraid to attempt?

6. What is your vision for yourself and your life if everything was ideal in every way?

7. What do you want people to say about you after you have passed on?

CHAPTER FIVE

How to Get the Job You Want—In Any Economy

*"*To be what we are, and to become what we are capable of becoming, is the only end of life.*"*
—ROBERT LOUIS STEVENSON

THIS IS THE GREATEST TIME in all of human history to be alive. There have never been more opportunities and possibilities for talented people in our economy than exist today.

The rate of new business formation in the United States has passed more than one million new companies per year. Millions of new jobs are being added in almost every industry. Unemployment levels are at an all-time low and employers everywhere are looking for talented, committed people to help their businesses grow.

The only real limit on business success today is the ability to attract and keep good people like you. More people are becoming financially successful today as a result of doing an excellent job and being paid well for it than ever before. Your job is to participate fully in the new economy and to realize your full potential by getting and keeping an excellent job and then moving upward and onward in your career for the rest of your working life.

I have personally worked in 22 different companies and industries. I have worked my way up into the position of chief operating officer of a $265 million company. In my various positions, I have not only applied for and gotten a series of jobs, but I have also hired numerous people for numerous positions in a variety of different industries performing a variety of different functions. In addition, I have worked as a consultant, trainer, and advisor to more than a thousand corporations throughout the United States, Canada, and worldwide. In this capacity, I have consulted and advised extensively on hiring practices and given insights and ideas to many executives that have enabled them to select the ideal people for their organizations.

Over the years, I have trained many thousands of men and women on the subject of Creative Job Search and taught them how to get good jobs, get better jobs, get paid more, and position themselves better for rapid advancement. Many graduates of my Creative Job Search programs went on to new or better jobs within days of completing the seminar.

In this chapter, I will share with you some of the very best ideas, strategies, methods, and techniques ever discovered for getting a great job in any economy. By applying these ideas and methods, you can put your career back onto the fast track.

TAKE CONTROL OF YOUR CAREER

This is the starting point of career success and maybe the most important point of all. Most people wander out into the job market, go on interviews, and then accept the best job that is offered to them. But this is not for you. Your goal is to take complete charge of your career from this moment forward.

With the rapid changes in the workplace, the average person starting work today will have 11 full-time jobs lasting two years or more and as many as four or five different careers over the course of his or her working lifetime. To weather these storms of lifelong career change, you must be proactive, not reactive. You must take complete control of your career and guide yourself into those industries and jobs that can give you the very best pay and the greatest opportunities for the future.

Self-directed job search enables you to take control of your career and your life. It puts you behind the wheel. It makes you the architect of your own destiny. It gives you a sense of control and develops a positive mental attitude.

SEE YOURSELF AS SELF-EMPLOYED

The starting point of taking control of your career, as I said, is to begin to view yourself as self-employed. See yourself as the president of a company with one employee: yourself. See yourself as having one product that you sell in a competitive marketplace: your personal services. See yourself as 100 percent responsible for your life and for everything that happens to you. Remember that no matter who signs your paycheck, you are always self-employed. The biggest mistake you can ever make is to ever think that you work for anyone else but yourself. You are always on your own payroll.

You are the president of your own personal-services corporation. Every day, every week, and every month you go into the marketplace and you sell the services of your own corporation to the highest bidder. As president of your own personal-services corporation, you are completely responsible for marketing yourself and for presenting yourself in the marketplace in the most attractive way. You are responsible for producing the highest quality and quantity of services of which you are capable. You are responsible for quality control and for doing excellent work in whatever is entrusted to you.

You are responsible for research and development and for continually upgrading your knowledge and skills so that you can do your job better and faster. You are responsible for finance and for organizing your financial life in such a way that you accomplish your financial goals. You are the president of your own company.

This attitude is the starting point of getting the job you want not only in the short term but for the rest of your career.

ANALYZE YOURSELF CAREFULLY

Before you go out and look for a job, you must sit down and take stock of yourself. You must look deeply into yourself and make some clear decisions about who you are and where you want to be in the future. It is only when you have a good understanding of yourself and your own desires and ambitions that you can go out and get the job you want.

Look into yourself and identify your most marketable skills. Make a list of all the things that you can do that someone in the marketplace would be willing to pay for. Here are some questions that you can ask and answer for yourself before you go to your first interview:

1. What are your basic skills? What can you do? What have you learned through education or experience that enables you to make a contribution and to get results that a company values and will pay for?

   1. _____

   2. _____

   3. _____

2. What have you done especially well at your various jobs in the past? What sorts of activities have been most responsible for your success in your work life up to now?

   1. _____

   2. _____

   3. _____

3. What sort of activities in your work and your personal life do you most enjoy? You will almost

always be most successful doing the things that you enjoy the most.

1. _____

2. _____

3. _____

4. What parts of your work do you do most easily and well? What you've done well in the past is often an indicator of what you would do best at in the future.

1. _____

2. _____

3. _____

IN MEDICINE, it is said that accurate diagnosis is half the cure. In your personal situation, accurate self-analysis—that is, taking the time to sit and think through the answers to these questions—is half the job of getting the ideal position for you.

The good news is that you will always do the very best at something that makes you the happiest. In fact, the situations in which you have been happy and successful in the past are the very best indications of where your true talents and abilities are. Your goal is to find a job doing something that enables you to use your very best, most developed qualities and abilities.

EXERCISES TO HELP YOU DETERMINE EXACTLY WHAT YOU WANT

Most people take whatever job is offered to them. They allow employers to determine the direction of their careers. Many people have never really given much thought to their careers since they took their first job. They have merely reacted to the demands placed upon them as the years went by. But this is not for you.

Here are ten exercises that you can practice throughout your career to make sure that you are on the right track.

1. Describe your ideal job. Remember you can't hit a target that you can't see. Imagine that you could do anything you want in the world. Exactly what would that job look like?

1. _____

2. _____

3. _____

2. Look around you in the marketplace. If you could have any job that you see, doing anything, what exactly would it be?

1. _____

2. _____

3. _____

If you do see a job that you like, phone or go and talk to someone who is doing that job and ask for the person's advice. You'll be amazed at the insights that people will give you in just a few minutes of conversation.

3. Project yourself into the future. What sort of work would you like to be doing in three to five years?

1. _____

2. _____

3. _____

Everyone has to start at the beginning in a new job or career, but you must be clear about where you want to be and what you want to be doing in the future. This enables you to make a much better decision with regard to taking a job in the first place.

4. If you could work anywhere in the country, taking into consideration weather and geography, where exactly would you like to work?

1. _____

2. _____

3. _____

Many people pack up and move to a different part of the country before taking a new job because that is where they have always wanted to live. Could this be true for you?

5. What size or type of company would you like to work for? Would you like to work for a small, medium, or large company? Would you like to work for a hi-tech or low-tech company? Would you like to work for a service or a manu-facturing company? Describe the ideal company for you in as much detail as you possibly can.

    1. _____

    2. _____

    3. _____

6. What kind of people would you like to work with? Describe your ideal boss. Describe your ideal colleagues. Remember, the quality of your co-workers and your social relationships at work are going to have more of an impact on your happiness and success than any other factor. Choose your boss and your colleagues with care. What kind of people would you like to work with and for?

    1. _____

    2. _____

    3. _____

7. How much would you like to earn? How much do you want to be earning in one year? Two years? Five years? This is very important. You should be asking questions about your earning ability and earnings ceiling at the job interview. Be sure that the job is at a company or in an industry

that enables you to achieve your earnings goals within the time horizon you've projected. What are your earnings targets?

1. _____

2. _____

3. _____

8. Who else is working at the kind of job that you would like to do or earning the kind of money that you would like to earn? What are they doing differently? What qualifications do they have that you still need to acquire?

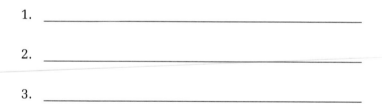

1. _____

2. _____

3. _____

9. Whom do you know who can help you position yourself for the kind of job you want? Who can give you advice? Who can point you in the right direction? Whom should you ask for help? Remember, everyone who succeeds does so with the help of other people.

1. _____

2. _____

3. _____

10. What level of responsibility do you desire? How high up do you want to rise in your career? What level or position would you be most comfortable with?

1. _____

2. _____

3. _____

THE MOST AMAZING THING IS THIS: The greater clarity you have about exactly what it is you want to do, where you want to do it, and how much you want to earn, the easier it is for someone to hire you and pay you the kind of money you want to make. Go back over these questions and answer them one by one before you go out looking for your next job.

THINK ABOUT THE FUTURE

More than 3,300 studies have found that one of the characteristics of leaders is that they have the ability to create a *vision*. This is something that you can develop by simply deciding to do so. You develop vision by projecting forward five or ten years into the future and thinking about how you would like your life to be if everything were ideal in every respect.

Here is an exercise that will help you develop "back from the future thinking." Imagine that five years have passed. Write out a description of what your career would look like if it were perfect in every way. Create a clear vision of your ideal job, company, and work environment. Write out how much you would be earning, what you would be doing, the kind of people you would be working with, and the level of responsibility you would have achieved.

Once you have a clear vision of your ideal future, ask yourself, "What would I have to do today to begin making my five-year vision a reality? What would have to happen?"

Leaders create a clear ideal picture for themselves and then they continually look for ways to make that ideal a reality. When you develop a clear vision for yourself and your future, the only question you then ask is, "How do I create this?" Failure is not an option.

How can you go about finding or creating the kind of job that you want where you can achieve your full potential? When you are clear about your vision for yourself and your future, you will be amazed at how much more likely you are to find the best job for you.

SET CLEAR GOALS FOR YOUR LIFE

Goal setting is the "Master Skill" of success. Success is goals and all else is commentary. When you are absolutely clear about your goals in every area of your life, the probabilities of your achieving those goals increases by several times.

This is a version of the seven-part goal-setting formula in Chapter 3. Once you learn this formula, you can practice it for the rest of your life. Here it is.

First, decide exactly what you want. Most people never do this. Decide exactly what you want in your career, and with your health, your finances, your family, and your future. You cannot hit a target that you can't see.

Second, write it down in clear, specific language. Only 3 percent of adults have clear, written goals, and they accomplish more than all the others put together. Remember, a goal that is not in writing is merely a wish or a fantasy. It has no energy behind it.

Third, set a deadline for your goal. If it is a large goal, set subdeadlines. Program your subconscious mind with a specific date upon which you wish to achieve your goal. Don't leave it hanging in the air.

Fourth, make a list of everything you can think of that you can do to achieve your goal. Think on paper. When you think of new things, keep adding them to your list until your list is complete.

Fifth, organize your list into a plan. Decide what you need to do first and what you can do later. Decide what is more important and what is less important. Once you have a goal and a plan, you will run circles around people who are just trying to figure things out as they go along.

Sixth, take action on your plan. Do something. Do anything. Put your plan into effect immediately. Hesitation and procrastination are the stumbling blocks upon which many of the greatest plans fail.

Seventh, and finally, do something every day that moves you toward your most important goal. Discipline yourself, every single day, to do something—anything—that moves you in the direction of what you want most at that time.

THE TEN-GOAL EXERCISE

Write down ten career goals that you want to accomplish in the next twelve months. Once you have these ten goals, put a circle around the one goal that is more important to you than any other single goal.

Transfer this goal to another sheet of paper. Write it down and set a deadline. Make a list of everything you can think of that you will have to do to achieve it. Organize the list into a plan, take action on the plan, and then do something every day to achieve that goal.

This goal-setting exercise can change your life almost overnight. It is the single most powerful process I have ever seen. Thousands of people worldwide tell me that their lives and careers were transformed, sometimes within a few days, by this seven-part goal-setting formula. Try it yourself and see.

UNDERSTAND THE JOB MARKET

There are certain principles of work and employment that are all basically facts of life. Some of these are practical and some of these are economic. They are principles that you have to take into consideration as long as you work for a living.

The first fact of work life is this: Your rewards in life, both tangible and intangible, will always be determined by the value of your service to other people. Your income will be determined by three things: (1) what you do, (2) how well you do it, and (3) the difficulty of replacing you. You can only ensure a higher income by doing something that is important, something for which there is a demand in the marketplace, and something in which you are difficult to replace.

A second fact of work life is that your labor, whatever you do, is a commodity in the marketplace. It is a factor of production. Your effort is a certain quantity of labor of a specific kind that can be applied to produce a certain quantity of products or services. All labor, including your own, is subject to the economic law of supply and demand.

YOUR SKILLS CAN BECOME OBSOLETE

A change in technology, market preferences by consumers, or the economy can make a particular skill obsolete almost overnight. A person who is fully employed and working 12 hours a day can find himself or herself out of work on Monday because of a rapid change in the marketplace, the company, or the demand for his or her work.

And here's the key point: Everybody works on *commission!* In a free society such as ours, everyone who works for a private business is on commission. Everyone receives a percentage of the sales and profits of the organization. No matter where you are in the organization, your salary or paycheck represents a part of the revenue generated by the company. And where there are no revenues, there are no paychecks. For this reason, the work you do is not determined so much by your background, your knowledge, your skills, or your ability as much as it is determined by what people need, and what people are willing to pay for.

You must be continually adjusting your offerings, your talents and skills, and your work and effort so that they conform to the needs of the current economy. Understanding this is essential for you to navigate the job market.

THE UNIVERSAL HIRING RULE

This is the great principle that gives you complete control over your career. The universal hiring rule simply says that wherever you can find an opportunity to increase revenues or to reduce costs in an amount greater than the cost of hiring you, you can actually create your own job.

The laws of economics state that an employer will continue to hire people as long as each additional person contributes more in dollar value to the company than that person costs in salary to the company. This means that you are surrounded with opportunities to create the kind of job you want by simply looking for ways to contribute more in value than you represent in cost. For the rest of your career, your salary will be determined by the financial impact that you have on your employer.

Perhaps the most important time-management principle is the Pareto principle, named after Italian economist Vilfredo Pareto, who developed it in 1895. This principle can be applied to the things that you do or can do for a company. The principle says that 20 percent of your activities account for 80 percent of the value of those activities. In fact, your ability to identify the most valuable and important things that you can do for an employer is the critical determinant of how fast you get the job you want, how much you get paid, and how rapidly you get promoted.

YOUR HIGHEST AND BEST USE

You have many different talents and abilities. Your responsibility is to think through and determine the few things that you can do that represent the highest and best use of your time for an employer. Sometimes, your ability to do a specific task in an excellent fashion can make you one of the most valuable and highest-paid people in the organization.

Thus, whenever you interview for a job or think about different jobs, you must continually analyze the jobs in terms of the most critical and valuable parts of them that you can do extremely well. One of the most important questions you should ask each day is, "How can I add more value to this particular job or position?"

When you have a job, or even before you get a job, you should be asking about and determining your highest value-added activities. And the more you can make your potential financial contribution clear to a prospective employer, the more rapidly he or she can hire you and put you to work. The universal hiring rule is also the universal rule for getting ahead in your career.

FISH WHERE THE FISH ARE

There are thousands of jobs available at any time in any economy, no matter what the economic situation. Even in times of high unemployment, usually more than 90 percent of people are working and earning good money. Most anyone who is really serious about getting and keeping a job can do so. There are no limitations. There are thousands of jobs around you that need to be done right now.

For example, every company, large or small, is a separate job market. There are approximately 50,000 companies per million people in the United States. Some of these companies are large and employ thousands of people. Most of them are small. But the fact remains that there is approximately one company, or one job market, for every 14 people in America.

In addition, every department in every company is a job market unto itself. Every department is like a small business. It has revenues and expenses. It has functions it must perform and responsibilities it must discharge. Every department hires and fires, advances and promotes, and deploys and utilizes different forms of labor.

MULTIPLE JOB MARKETS

Every individual in every department in every company who has the authority to hire people is also a job market.

Even in a company with as few as 20 people, there are four or five individuals who have the authority to hire others. Each of these four or five people is a job market unto itself, with specific needs and requirements, with problems unsolved and needs unmet.

This means that in every city or town, in every economy, there are literally thousands of companies, departments, or individuals who are job markets and who have varying levels of needs for specific services. Your job is to find the right one for you.

Remember, a job is merely a problem that is not yet solved. A job is an opportunity to render useful service, to help someone fulfill a need, or to achieve a goal. Whenever you can find a person with a problem or an opportunity, you can create your own full-time or part-time job.

Read the newspapers and magazines advertising job openings. Check the Internet regularly. Speak to placement agencies and executive recruiters. Cast a wide net. And always remember, there are vastly more jobs available than skilled and talented people to take them.

USE YOUR TIME WELL

When you start looking for a new job, you must accept complete responsibility for using every minute of every day in the very best way possible. You should look upon your job search as a full-time job, taking 40 to 50 hours each week, starting first thing in the morning and continuing all day long. The more active you are, the more people you see, the more information you get, and the more opportunities you investigate, the more likely it is that you are going to get a far better job than a person who waits at home for someone to call or who goes out on an occasional job interview.

Remember, you are the president of your own company. As the president, you are responsible for every aspect of your company's operations. You are responsible for planning, organizing, setting priorities, delegating, self-supervision, and especially, you are responsible for getting results.

Get up each morning and plan each day in advance. Make a list of everything you have to do that day and organize the list by priority. Select the most important item on the list and begin with it immediately. All day long, work from your list and challenge yourself to get through everything as quickly as you possibly can.

SEE YOURSELF AS FULLY EMPLOYED

Arise early, exactly as if you were fully employed. Get up, get dressed exactly as if you were going to work, and then get ready to go. Eat a light, high-energy breakfast. Go to the table or desk that you have set aside as a workplace for your job search and get on the telephone. Make your first call by 8:30 a.m. Whenever possible, schedule your first appointment for early morning, even before regular working hours.

Getting up, getting dressed, and looking good not only increases your self-confidence and improves your attitude, but it positively impresses other people, both those inside your own house and those on the outside. Remember, you should never see yourself as unemployed. You are merely a fully employed person who is in a temporary state of transition.

Ask yourself the key question, "What is the most valuable use of my time right now?" And whatever the answer is to that question, be sure that you are working on that every single minute.

The final and most important question in getting the job you want is to continually ask yourself, "Is what I am doing right now leading to a job interview or a job?" Do not drop off your dry cleaning, pick up your laundry, read the newspaper, watch television, or chat with your friends during work hours. See yourself as fully employed at getting a position in which you are fully employed. Don't waste time. Develop a sense of urgency. Move quickly. Cover as much ground as you possibly can every single day. Use your time well every single minute.

DO YOUR HOMEWORK

When you are looking for the job you want, you are in the same situation as a professional salesperson. You are selling all day long.

The three keys to sales success are prospecting, presenting, and following up. Your job is to prospect thoroughly and to develop the greatest number of leads that you possibly can. Then, meet with and make presentations to as many prospective employers as possible. Third, follow up with the very best opportunities until you get the job you want.

One of the most important keys to success in selling today is what is called precall research. This means that you find out everything that you possibly can about a prospective employer before you call on that employer. Fortunately, with the Internet, you can do more and better research in a few minutes than has ever before been possible in human history. You cannot imagine how impressive it is when a job candidate calls on a person and has a file full of information on that individual, organization, and industry. It builds credibility instantly and gives you a critical edge in the final decision. This winning edge can open a door for you that can change the entire direction of your life.

Do your homework. Find out everything that you possibly can about the individual, the organization, and the industry before you call on them the first time. This is very impressive!

PREPARE THOROUGHLY IN ADVANCE

In professional selling, the difference between the amateur and the professional is summarized in what is called precall planning. This means that you take a few minutes in the morning to develop your plan for this interview. You review all the information you have on this industry, this organization, and this person. You develop a series of questions that you want to ask. You review what is going on in the industry and both the types of jobs and the potential incomes that are possible. You read the newspapers and you check the Internet to find out what competitive organizations are doing and offering.

Preparation is the mark of the professional. It is absolutely amazing to me how many people have applied for positions in my company but have no idea what my company does. They somehow think that they are such good talkers that they can get away with fast talk and phoniness to cover up the fact that they have not spent any time preparing for the interview. Don't let this happen to you.

Put yourself in the position of the employer. Think through what the employer will need to know in order to offer you the kind of job that you really want. The better prepared you are, the more impressive you will appear and the easier it will be for someone to hire you.

SOW SEEDS EVERYWHERE

Fully 85 percent of the jobs available in your market are not advertised or publicized anywhere. This is called the hidden job market. They are not posted on any employee bulletin board. They are not advertised in the newspaper. They are hidden and waiting for you to discover them, like buried treasure.

Perhaps the most important part of the hidden job market today is the Internet. Though virtually nothing a few years ago, the Internet is now home to approximately one-eighth of all job advertisements. You should not only surf the Internet job sites regularly, you should also make sure that your qualifications and your interests are on every job site that might be visited by employers who are looking for someone like you.

Getting a job via the Internet is not easy. It is a skill that you can learn through practice. You start by visiting the main Internet job sites that you see advertised. If you don't know where to start, go to a search engine like Google or Yahoo and click on Jobs and Job Opportunities. Visit AOL and go to the employment section. Craigslist.com has become increasingly popular for job seekers. Examine the various job categories and read the descriptions of the jobs that are being offered.

Get as much information as you possibly can about the various job sites. Some Internet job sites specialize in one kind of employee and some specialize in another. Some are local and some are national. When you list yourself on an Internet job site, your résumé and your information become instantly available to potential employers nationwide.

There are many free opportunities for you to post a brief description of your abilities and the job you are looking for at no charge. Some sites do charge a listing fee, but they are usually worth it because they are much more aggressive in attracting potential employers to the site. Remember, you generally get what you pay for in life.

There are also job fairs held in every community each year. These are advertised in the newspaper and on the radio. Visit these job fairs and talk to the various employers exhibiting there. Find out what they are looking for today and what they will be looking for in the future. Even if you are currently employed, keep sowing seeds everywhere you go so that you can prepare for a rich harvest of employment in the future. The more seeds you sow the more likely you are to get the job you really want.

INCREASE THE PROBABILITY OF SUCCESS

Your success in getting a great job is a numbers game. It is based on the law of averages. It is based on probability. It simply means that the more people you see and talk to, the greater the probability that you will be in the right place, at the right time, with the right person and the right opportunity to get the job you want.

To increase the likelihood of getting a great job, read the newspapers in your city carefully. Especially study the business and career sections. Read with a red pen or a highlighter in hand and make careful notes for follow-up. Make it a point to be aware of the trends in business in the city in which you wish to work.

You should also read the trade publications in your field or in the field in which you desire to work. You can subscribe to these, buy them at your local magazine stand, or find them at your local library. Often they are available at no charge on the Internet.

When you begin interviewing and asking around for a job, ask people what magazines or publications cover that particular field. When you read these magazines, look for stories about companies that are growing, expanding, or engaging in innovative activities. Remember, heightened business activity creates demand for new people.

Read all the business magazines, both local and national, keeping an eye out for stories about companies and trends in the industry in which you wish to work. Read the local business journal from cover to cover and look for the companies that are announcing new positions or introducing new products or services. Business journals usually contain information on jobs that are available as well as people who are moving up within their existing companies.

SEEK OUT KEY PEOPLE

Look for the names of key people in various companies and departments of companies. Especially look for the names of those who have been recently promoted. People who have been recently promoted often make immediate staff changes and create job opportunities for people who call.

Look for active, growing organizations that are announcing new expansions or increased profitability. These companies are always looking for more good people. They offer lots of opportunities and they pay well. Look for new product releases and the introductions of new services. Wherever a company is expanding its products or services, there are job opportunities to sell the product, distribute the product, service the product, install the product, and handle the administration and details associated with the new product or service. These represent new job opportunities.

Whenever you see a company that is expanding and an executive that has been promoted, phone the company immediately and tell the person you talk to that you are looking for a job in that industry and this company is of interest to you. Ask the receptionist to transfer you to the new executive. He or she is probably not yet receiving many phone calls. Arrange to go in and see the person and interview for a job.

It is absolutely amazing how many great job opportunities you can uncover by simply taking action on the news and information all around you about the business and industry that you want to work in.

THE THREE Cs TO GETTING ANY JOB

There are three basic components to getting the kind of job you want and earning the kind of money you want. These three elements stay constant throughout your working career. They are contacts, credibility, and competence.

1. *Contacts.* The more contacts you have in the marketplace, the more likely you are to find the job you want. The more people you know and who know you, the more likely you are to uncover the 85 percent or more of job openings that are never listed anywhere.

This is why it is so important for you to network continually. Join clubs and associations. Ask people for referrals and references. Tell your friends, relatives, and associates that you are in the market for a new job. Make sure that everyone you know is aware that you are available and are looking for a job. Nothing can be more important than your circle of contacts.

The great majority of jobs that are filled in the hidden job market are filled because of someone who knows someone else. And you can expand your range of contacts just by telling people that you are available and asking for their help and their advice.

2. *Credibility.* This is a combination of your reputation and your character. Credibility is your single most important quality in terms of getting recommendations and referrals from your contacts.

Make sure that everything you do is honest and consistent with the highest ethical standards. Make sure that you never say or do anything that could be misconstrued as anything other than excellent conduct on your part. Remember, people will only recommend you for a job opening if they are completely confident that they will not end up looking foolish as a result of something you do or say.

3. *Competence.* In the final analysis, it is how good you are and how good you have been in your previous jobs that will determine, more than anything else, how good you will be perceived to be at the job under consideration.

Your level of competence will be the single most important factor in determining your career success. This is why you must continually work to maintain and upgrade your levels of competence and skill through personal and professional development activities all your working life.

THE FIVE QUALITIES MOST IN DEMAND

Every employer has had a certain amount of experience with both good employees and bad employees. For this reason every employer has a pretty good idea of what he or she wants more of and less of. Here are the big five.

The first quality that employers look for is *intelligence*. More than one study has found that intelligence is responsible for 76 percent of an employee's productivity and contribution. Intelligence in this sense means the ability to plan, to organize, to set priorities, to solve problems, and to get the job done.

Intelligence also refers to your level of common sense or practical ability to deal with the day-to-day challenges of the job. The way you demonstrate your intelligence is by asking intelligent questions. Curiosity is a hallmark of intelligence. The more you ask good questions and listen to the answers, the smarter you appear and become.

The second quality sought by employers is *leadership ability*. Leadership is the willingness and the desire to accept responsibility for results. It's the ability to take charge, to volunteer for assignments, and to accept accountability for achieving the required results of those assignments.

The mark of a leader is that he or she does not make excuses. You demonstrate your willingness and ability to be a leader in the organization by offering to take charge of achieving company goals and then committing yourself to performing at high levels.

Integrity is the third quality sought by employers. It's probably the single most important quality for long-term success in life and at work. Integrity begins by being true to yourself. This means that you are perfectly honest with yourself and your relationships with others. You are willing to admit your strengths and weaknesses. You are willing to admit where you have made mistakes in the past. Especially, you demonstrate loyalty. You never say anything negative about a previous employer or person with whom or for whom you have worked. Even if you were fired from a previous job, never say anything negative or critical.

The fourth quality that employers look for is *likeability*. Employers prefer people who are warm, friendly, easy-going, and cooperative with others. Employers are looking for people who can join the team and be part of the work family. Men and women with good personalities are almost always more popular and more effective at whatever they do.

Teamwork is the key to modern business success. Your experience in working as part of a team in the past, and your willingness to work as part of a team in the future, can be one of the most attractive things about you to prospective employers.

Competence is the fifth quality sought by employers. Competence is terribly important to your success. It is really the foundation quality of everything that happens to you in your career. In its simplest terms, competence means the ability to get the job done. Competence means the ability to set priorities, to determine the most important things to do, to separate the relevant from the irrelevant, and then to concentrate single-mindedly on the most important task until the job is complete.

In the final analysis, it is your character, which is the sum total of all your positive qualities, that will have the greatest impact on whether you get the job you want. Your job is to continue working on your character by practicing the behaviors of top people at every opportunity.

WRITE RÉSUMÉS THAT GET RESULTS

Your résumé is a combination sales and promotion tool. Just as a company produces brochures and promotional materials for its products and services, your résumé is your promotional tool for yourself. It is a way of presenting yourself as a person who can perform specific duties and services. As an advertising piece, your résumé must be interesting, inviting, factual, attractive, positive, and upbeat. It must entice the reader to want to meet you, talk to you, and learn more about how you can perhaps help him or her to achieve his or her goals.

The fact is that it usually requires a large number of résumés to get a single job offer. It turns out that very few people are ever hired simply because of a résumé. It is like a business card. Many people are actually hired without their résumés ever being read in the first place.

The ideal length of a résumé is one page, with a maximum of two pages. People today are extremely busy and they don't have time to read long documents. Therefore, make your résumé short and to the point.

TWO TYPES OF RÉSUMÉS

There are two types of résumés: chronological and functional. The chronological résumé lists your previous job experiences with the most recent at the top of the résumé. The résumé goes back month by month and year by year, describing your work experience and education from the beginning of your adult life.

You use a chronological résumé when you've had a career path that shows consistent growth and development. A chronological résumé is best when you started with a simple job and then moved up gradually to more complex jobs. A functional résumé, on the other hand, groups your experience by skill, job function, or previous achievements. It is helpful to use a functional résumé when you have spent a good deal of time with a single company but have performed a variety of different tasks within that company.

In a functional résumé, you identify the various job functions that you have performed. You list your accomplishments and achievements in each of these job areas. For example, if you started with a company and worked up from a lower position to a higher position, you would start off by listing your title in the highest position and the things you accomplished. You would then list your title in the second position and the things you accomplished in that job.

TRANSFERABILITY OF RESULTS

The most important part of a résumé or a job interview is called *transferability of results*. What employers are looking for is *proof* that you have already achieved the results that they need.

Ideally, you should avoid giving an employer your résumé until after you have had a personal interview. Whenever possible, avoid mailing your résumé in advance.

If, however, you are responding to an advertisement and you have no choice but to mail your résumé, always send it with a cover letter that refers specifically to the advertisement and to the job for which you are seeking. Even if your letter is handwritten, you should send it as a cover letter with the résumé.

Finally, once you have either sent your résumé or left your résumé behind, be sure to follow up with a phone call in a couple of days to hear the reaction. Don't be afraid to be persistent as long as you are polite. Employers generally consider persistence a positive attribute.

PREPARE THOROUGHLY FOR THE INTERVIEW

There are several things that you can do to make each interview as successful as it can possibly be. Each of these steps will have a significant impact on helping you to get the kind of job you really want.

1. *Always be punctual.* Allow yourself enough time to get there, taking the address and the traffic into consideration. As a general rule, employers never hire a person who arrives late for a job interview.

2. *Dress well for the interview.* Your clothes can account for 95 percent of the first impression you make on your prospective employer, because first impressions are almost always visual. Dress the way you would expect to dress for the job for which you are applying. Many people are hired for no other reason than that they are the best-dressed candidates.

3. *Before going into the interview, take a few moments to breathe deeply and relax your shoulders.* Breathing deeply six or seven times will actually release endorphins in your brain and give you a heightened sense of well-being and calmness.

4. *After breathing deeply, close your eyes for a few moments and visualize yourself as calm, confident, and relaxed.* Create a clear mental picture of yourself as smiling, positive, and completely in control of yourself and your emotions during the interview.

5. *When you meet the interviewer, smile and shake hands firmly.* Look the person directly in the eye and say, "How do you do?" A good handshake is full and firm, where you grasp the entire hand and squeeze in a firm but nonaggressive way. Both men and women should give a full-palm handshake when they meet a person for the first time.

6. *Interview the interviewer.* Most interviewers start off with a series of questions that are aimed at drawing you out and getting a better idea of who you are. You should instead take control of the interview by asking questions about the company, the industry, and the kind of person the interviewer is looking for.

The more questions you ask and the more you focus on uncovering the real needs of the prospective employer, the more likely it is that the prospective employer will see you as being the kind of person who can fulfill those needs.

INTERVIEW LIKE A CHAMPION

The job interview is really a sales call. When you are looking for a job, you're in sales. You are going out to sell yourself to someone else. The type of job you get and the type of salary you command will be a measure of how well you have sold yourself at this critical point in your career.

Many people don't like the idea of selling. They don't like to see themselves as salespeople. Unfortunately, this is the type of attitude that leads to underachievement in life. The fact is that people who want to sell their ideas or themselves to others are salespeople. The only question is whether you are any good at it.

Every employer has needs that are not yet satisfied. Every employer has problems that are not yet solved. Every employer represents an opportunity for you. In many cases, employers will actually create jobs for people who can satisfy needs and solve problems.

EMPLOYERS ARE COMPLETELY SELFISH: GIVE THEM WHAT THEY NEED

Your prospective employer has only one question in mind when interviewing you for a job. It is the same question that every customer asks when considering whether to buy a product or service. And your employer is a customer. You are the product or service that is for sale. And your prospective customer's question is: "What's in it for me?"

Your prospective employer is thinking, "How will I personally benefit from hiring you?" He or she is asking, "What can you do for me, specifically?" And finally, your prospective employer is silently asking, "How can I be sure that what you say is true?"

Your aim in the job interview is to demonstrate that you can *achieve, avoid, or preserve* something for your employer. You must be absolutely clear about what it is you expect to achieve, avoid, or preserve. Your other key goal in a job interview is to convince the employer that you can achieve a result that he or she needs, or improve a situation that he or she is facing, at less than the cost of hiring you. The better you plan and prepare, the better you will be at convincing the employer that you are the ideal person for this job.

INFORMATIONAL INTERVIEWING

Informational interviewing is the key to creative job search. When you interview for hire, you are the interviewee. You sit there and the prospective employer asks you questions and grills you about your background and ability.

However, in informational interviewing, you are the *interviewer.* You have control over the interview. You are actually screening the employer rather than being screened by the employer. You can ask hard questions about the business and the industry without worrying about whether you make a good impression.

Some form of informational interviewing is used by virtually everyone who gets a good job with high wages in a short period of time. It is one of the most powerful job-seeking techniques ever discovered, and it will work for you if you practice it.

PREPARE THOROUGHLY

You begin by making a list of prospective companies that you would like to work for. You then identify one of these companies and gather information about both the company and the person in the company whom you want to talk to. Study the company website and download it so that you can make notes. At the very least, telephone the receptionist and say you are a potential customer. Ask him or her to send you a complete package of promotional literature on the company and its products and services.

Then phone and ask for an appointment with the right person. Tell the person, either by phone, voice mail, e-mail, or letter, that you would like to *interview* him or her to get some ideas about working in this particular field. Say, "I'm doing some research in this industry. I'm thinking of making a career change into this field and I am talking to several authorities in this industry to get some information and ideas on how to make the best choice." Surprisingly enough, people who are normally too busy to talk to you or who do not have the time for interviews will actually make time to give advice to someone who is looking to move into and up in an industry in which they work.

Tell the prospective employer, "I would like to interview you for about ten minutes and ask you some specific questions." People usually love to be interviewed. And if you ask for only ten minutes, you will almost invariably get an appointment within a few days.

You are now the interviewer. Before you go to the interview, create a list of about seven questions about the industry and the company. In the interview, thank the employer for his time, and then ask these questions about the industry, the company, the prospects for the future, and the prospects for different people in different jobs. Make careful notes during your interview. At the end of ten minutes, be prepared to thank the individual and depart. Almost invariably, you will be invited to stay longer.

Never accept or respond to a job offer during the informational interview. If the employer asks you if you are looking for a job, you respond by saying, "No, not at this time. I am still in the process of doing my research and I'm not far enough along to make that kind of a decision."

After the interview, immediately go home and write a thank-you note. This is a powerful part of the informational interviewing process and it virtually guarantees your ability to go back at a later time with your findings.

GETTING THE JOB

You have done your research and your informational interviewing. You have met with the prospective employer and you have sent your follow-up thank-you letters. You have researched the company and the industry, and you have taken complete control of your career. You have now decided where you want to work and for whom you want to work. You are now ready to close the sale.

Telephone the employer who, on the basis of your research, you have decided you want to work for. Say, "I have completed my research on this industry and I would like to show you what I have found." When you meet with the prospective employer, explain that, of all the companies you have researched, *this* is the place you would like to work. Then explain why. Then go over your findings about the industry and tell him or her why *this* is the best company, with the best future, and exactly how you and your special skills can help this company be even more successful in the future.

THE POWER OF SELF-SELECTION

Perhaps the most powerful tool of all in a job interview is called self-selection. It's the fact that you really want the job. Your intense desire for the job, demonstrated by everything you say or do, is extremely impressive and influential in getting you the job you want.

When you are closing the sale for the job you want, your job is to convince the employer overwhelmingly that this is the right job for you and that you are the right person for this job. Describe your experience as it relates to the position. Describe what you feel you could do for the employer. Explain the contribution you feel you could make to the prospective employer and to the company. Don't be afraid to be enthusiastic and assertive in "selling yourself" to the prospective employer.

Be active, direct, and straightforward in the interview. Smile, nod, and make it clear that you are fully involved in the discussion. Show that you are really eager to get this job with this company and with this person. Especially, *tell* the prospective employer that you really want this job. There is probably nothing that you can say that is more impressive to a prospective employer than, "I really want this job. If you give me a chance at this job, I promise you I will do a terrific job in this position. You won't be sorry." Sometimes, this is impressive enough to cause the person to hire you rather than someone else.

Remember, employers are emotional, and emotions are contagious. Your excitement and enthusiasm for a job can have a greater impact on the employer's decision than all the résumés you ever write. Your success in persuading the employer that you are the right person will determine the quality of the job you get and the salary that goes with that job, as much as or more than any other factor.

NEGOTIATING THE BEST SALARY

You have interviewed and successfully persuaded the employer that he or she should hire you for the job. You now come to the issue of salary negotiations. What you do at this point can have a major impact on your income, your lifestyle, and your future. Follow these instructions carefully.

First, you should have a good idea of how much you want to earn in this position. You should have done your research and spoken to other people. You should know what the salary range is for a position of this kind. You should never go in blind, having no idea of how much money to ask for.

Whatever salary is offered to you, never accept either the job or the salary the first time it comes up. Always ask for time to think it over, even if you want this job very badly. Use the 24-hour rule: Always allow yourself, and ask for, 24 hours to think about a job offer before you accept it. If you ask for time to think it over, the better job and job benefits you are going to get when you make the final decision.

DETERMINE THE SALARY RANGE

When an employer offers you a salary, he or she usually has a salary range in mind. The salary range is usually 20 percent above and below the average amount paid for that position. For example, if a position pays roughly $2,000 per month, the employer will be thinking in the range of $1,600 (20 percent below) to $2,400 (20 percent above) per month.

The employer will make every effort to hire you at the lowest possible amount that you will accept. Your job, on the other hand, is to aim for the very highest amount that the employer is prepared to pay. Your job is to ask for an amount at the top of the salary range in the employer's mind.

Here is how you do it. When an employer offers you a salary of $2,000 per month, for example, you should suggest a figure that is between 110 percent and 130 percent of that amount. This is called bracketing. In this example, if the suggested figure is $2,000, you should say that you feel that excellent performance in this position would be worth between $2,200 and $2,600. You raise the limits of the bracket in the employer's mind and in the conversation.

Surprisingly enough, the employer will often settle for an amount that is midway between the two figures that you are proposing, or in this example, $2,400. This is the upper end of his or her salary range, and it is usually more than he or she planned to pay, but the employer will often give it to you if you ask for it in this way.

AGREE ON THE TERMS OF A SALARY INCREASE

In some cases, you will have to settle for a lower salary to start. In that case, you immediately ask what you will have to do to get an increase in salary. Be specific and ask the employer to put these terms in the job offer letter to you.

If you cannot get a higher salary, you can negotiate the benefits that come with the job. You can negotiate for a longer vacation, for example, and receive more days off and more sick days. In addition, you can ask for more perks, such as an office, a car, an expense account, and other things.

In any case, whatever salary, benefits, and package you negotiate, immediately ask if you can get an increase within 90 days if you do a good job. Your ability to negotiate for a better package at a higher salary later is better at the moment of taking the job than it ever will be again.

Be sure to take lots of time to think through and discuss all the details involved in the job. Make sure you understand and write down every agreed-upon term. You will then be ready to put your career onto the fast track.

NO-LIMIT THINKING

The thought that you put into your career and into the job you get will have as much of an impact on your life as any other decision or series of actions you ever take. It is vitally important that you become absolutely excellent at conducting a creative job search and that you review and practice these ideas over and over again until they become habits that you practice for the rest of your life.

Remember, you are a truly excellent person. You are engineered for success and designed to have a wonderful career in the months and years ahead. Getting the kind of job you want is both an art and a science. It is a learnable skill that you can develop by reviewing this chapter over and over again and then by taking action on what you have learned. There are no limits to what you can accomplish in life—except for the limits you place on yourself.

QUESTIONS FOR REFLECTION

1. What are the best jobs you have ever had, where you were the happiest and felt most fulfilled?

2. What did your best jobs, and best parts of those jobs, have in common?

3. If you could be guaranteed success at getting and doing well in any job, what job would you go after?

4. What kinds of people, as employers, co-workers, and customers, do you most enjoy working with?

5. Imagine that you could wave a magic wand and create the perfect job for you; what would it look like?

6. Where do you want to be in your career in five years, and what additional skills and knowledge will you have to have at that time to be successful?

7. What is the first thing you should do as the result of your answers to these questions, and what you have learned in this chapter?

CHAPTER **SIX**

How Do You Get Ahead?

*"*What is the recipe for successful achievement? To my mind there are just four essential ingredients: Choose a career you love, give it the best there is in you, seize your opportunities, and be a member of the team.*"*

—BENJAMIN F. FAIRLESS, CHAIRMAN AND CEO OF U.S. STEEL (1952–1955)

IN THIS CHAPTER, you will learn a series of practical, proven, simple, and effective ways to get paid more money for what you do and get promoted faster to higher levels of authority and responsibility.

These methods and techniques are used by the highest-paid and most successful people in our society. When you begin to use them yourself, you will put your entire life and career onto the fast track. You will make more progress in the next few years than the average person makes in 10 or 20 years of just plodding along with the crowd.

Your choice of a career, and a job within that career, is one of the most important decisions you ever make. Unfortunately, most people drift into their jobs, accepting whatever is offered to them at the time and then allowing other people to determine what they will do, where they will do it, how they will do it, and how much they will be paid for it. The company and the boss become very much like an extension of the mother and the father. There begins a natural inertia and momentum that carries most people onward through their careers, month after month, and year after year.

GET PAID MORE AND PROMOTED FASTER

But by now you've learned that this is not for you. Your goal is to get a great job that you really enjoy and that pays you the very most that you can possibly earn in exchange for your mental, emotional, and physical energies. The good news is that, no matter what your situation, you are not trapped. You have free will. You have choices. There are countless things that you can do with your talents and abilities, and there are numerous places where you will be appreciated more, paid at a higher rate, and promoted faster than you ever have up until now.

Because of the dynamism and the rapid rate of change in our economy, a person starting work today will have many different jobs in his/her career. *Fortune* magazine reported recently that more than 40 percent of the population will be contingency workers or "free agents" for much of their careers. That is, they will seldom have a long-term, lifelong job with a single company or organization.

YOU WORK FOR YOURSELF

One of the biggest mistakes you can ever make is to ever think that you work for anyone else but yourself. We have moved from an era of lifelong employment to an era of lifelong *employability*. No matter who signs your paycheck, you are your own boss, completely responsible for every part of your work and personal life. In the long run, you determine how much you get paid and everything that happens to you. You are responsible.

The top 3 percent of Americans view themselves as self-employed, no matter where the work and no matter who signs their paycheck. This attitude of self-employment makes them more valuable to their companies and, as a result, they get paid more and promoted faster.

From now on, see yourself as a consultant or free agent to your existing company, determined to justify the amount they are paying you every single day.

DECIDE EXACTLY WHAT YOU WANT

This is perhaps the most important step of all in your career. Take the time to analyze your personal talents and abilities.

Look deep into yourself to decide what it is that you really enjoy doing. What are the activities that interest you and hold your attention? In the past, what have been your peak experiences and your most enjoyable moments?

You have been designed by nature to do certain things and perform certain tasks extraordinarily well. You have been engineered for success from the very beginning. You have within you deep reservoirs of talent and ability that you have never tapped into up until now. You have the capacity to be, have, and do virtually anything that you can put your mind to. But you must accept the responsibility of deciding exactly what it is you want and then dedicating yourself wholeheartedly to achieving those goals.

PRACTICE ZERO-BASED THINKING

Here is a great thinking tool for you. For the rest of your life, practice *zero-based thinking* in everything you do. Zero-based thinking requires that you draw a line under all of your previous decisions up until now and ask yourself this question: "Is there anything in my life that I am doing today that, knowing what I now know, I wouldn't get into again today, if I had to do it over again?"

The fact is that in times of turbulence and rapid change, and for the rest of your life, you will always have at least one answer to this question. There will always be at least one thing that you are doing, that, knowing what you now know, you wouldn't get into again, if you had to do it over.

How can you tell if you are in a "zero-based thinking" situation? It's simple: It's called *stress*. Whenever you experience chronic stress, unhappiness, anger, or dissatisfaction of any kind, it is almost always because you are in a situation that, knowing what you now know, you wouldn't get into again today if you had to do it over.

Apply zero-based thinking to your current or most recent job. Knowing what you now know, would you take this job again, under the terms and conditions that you are now working? Would you take this job and work for this particular boss? Would you go to work for this company? In this industry? At this salary? Or in this position? If the answer is no, your next questions are, "How do I get out of this situation, how fast, and how do I avoid getting into this situation again?"

REVIEW EACH PART OF YOUR LIFE

You can also apply zero-based thinking to each part of your life. Apply it to your relationships: Is there any relationship in your life, personal or business, that knowing what you now know, you wouldn't get into again today if you had to do it over?

Is there any investment of time, money, or emotion that is holding you back or weighing you down, that knowing what you now know, you wouldn't get into again today?

The reason zero-based thinking is so important is that until you deal with the dissatisfactions of the present, you cannot move onward and upward to create the wonderful future that is possible for you. In deciding what you want, imagine that you could have any job at all. Imagine that all jobs and positions are open to you. Imagine that there is a job out there that you would really enjoy doing, hour after hour and day after day. One of the great success secrets is for you to decide what you really enjoy doing and then to find a job doing that one thing or combination of things.

THE HAPPINESS TEST

It is interesting to note that you will always be paid more and promoted faster when you are doing something that makes you happy, something that fills you with joy and satisfaction. In fact, unless your work really makes you happy, you will never be able to develop the commitment, passion, and dedication necessary to rise above the difficulties, challenges, and setbacks that every job or career contains.

And when deciding what you really want in a job, be purely selfish. Listen only to yourself, to your inner voice. Decide what you would really enjoy doing personally before you start thinking about what might be possible.

My brother left high school and worked at odd jobs for a couple of years. One day, he decided that he wanted to become a landscape architect. He spent the next three and a half years in a technical school learning landscape architecture. He worked with landscape architects on the weekends and during the summer. Finally, he got his degree.

Two years later, he realized that landscape architecture was not what he had expected. Instead, he decided that he wanted to be a lawyer. He was clear that this was the career for him. It took him five more years of hard work in night school and his afternoons and weekends before he managed to get a degree in law. Today, he has a thriving legal practice, he is doing work that he really enjoys, and he is making a wonderful living.

The point is this: You may have to put in a lot of effort and make a lot of false starts before you find the ideal career for you. But it all starts with you sitting down and deciding what it is you really want and then getting started.

SELECT THE RIGHT INDUSTRY AND THE RIGHT COMPANY

Each year, and in each economic cycle, some industries are growing and expanding and absorbing many thousands of people. These industries are offering incredible opportunities for men and women who want to get ahead more rapidly than the average person.

At the same time, other industries have flattened out or are actually declining. These industries continue to hire to replace the workers that they are losing, but as a result of automation, technology, changing consumer preferences, and competition, these industries are not likely to grow in the years ahead. Your job is to begin by separating the high-growth industries from the low-growth industries.

You can make more progress, get paid more, and get promoted faster in a high-growth industry or a fast-growing company in a couple of years than you might in five or ten years in a slow-growth or declining industry.

IDENTIFY THE TOP 20 PERCENT

Once you have identified a high-growth industry, do your homework. Find out which companies in that industry are growing the most rapidly. Remember, 20 percent of companies in any industry make 80 percent of the money and 80 percent of the profits. They have better leadership, better market positions, better technology, and better futures. These are the companies where you want to work.

See yourself and your skills as a valuable resource, like money, and view the market as a place where you are going to invest yourself to get the very highest return on your mental, emotional, and physical energies. Be purely selfish when it comes to committing your life and your work to a particular company in a particular industry.

A woman came up to me in one of my seminars recently and asked me what she could do to get paid more and promoted faster in her current job. I asked her what she was doing. She told me that she was working for a manufacturing company. As it happens, the company had tough competition from the Japanese, who offered similar products at lower prices with equal or better quality. As a result, the company had not grown in 10 years. I told her that there was very little future in a company or an industry that was in decline. If she was really serious about getting ahead in her career and in her life, she should join a faster-growing company in a more dynamic industry.

She wrote to me later to tell me that she had taken my advice. She was now earning 40 percent more after one year with a new company than she was earning after several years with the old company. Not only that, she had been promoted twice and was on the fast track in her career.

LOOK FOR THE BEST REPUTATION

According to Theodore Levitt, an influential economic scholar and former dean of Harvard Business School, the most valuable asset that a company has is its reputation. Reputation is defined as how a company is known to its customers. If you are interested in working in a particular industry, ask around and find out which companies have the best reputations for quality, service, innovation, and leadership. Even within your own company, parts of the company may be growing and expanding while other parts of the company may have leveled off or are declining. Your goal should be to invest yourself where the best future is possible for you.

J. Paul Getty, the great oil billionaire, once wrote a book on success titled *How to Be Rich*. In it, he recommended that you find a company that you want to work in and then go to that company and be willing to take any job it offers you. Get your foot in the door. Once you are inside, you will have a chance to perform and to move up rapidly. This is a good strategy.

SELECT THE RIGHT BOSS

This is one of the most important decisions that you ever make. Choosing the right boss can help your career and help you get paid more and promoted faster than almost anything else you do.

Look upon accepting a job as the equivalent of entering into a business marriage, with your boss as your spouse.

He or she is going to have an enormous impact on how much you get paid, how much you enjoy your work, how rapidly you get promoted, and every other part of your work life.

When you are looking for a job, you should interview your boss carefully to make sure that this is the kind of person you would enjoy working with. This should be someone whom you could respect and look up to. This must be someone who is friendly and supportive and on whom you can depend to help you move ahead as rapidly as possible in your own career.

It's a good idea to talk to other people who work for that boss. Check his or her background. Ask around and see if you can find someone who knows him or her personally and who will give you a candid assessment of the person.

QUALITIES OF THE BEST BOSSES

The best bosses have certain qualities in common. First of all, they have high *integrity*. When they make a promise, they keep it. When they say they will do something, they do it exactly as they said. When they promise you a review or an increase, they follow through, right on schedule.

The best bosses also take the time to be *clear* when they delegate a task to you. They discuss it with you and ensure that you know exactly what you are expected to do, and when, and to what standard of quality.

The best bosses are *considerate* and *caring* about their people. They are interested in you as a person as well as in you as an employee. They want to know about your personal life, your family, your spouse, and children. They want to know about the things that concern you and that affect the way you think and feel at work. This doesn't mean that a good boss is a father or mother, confessor, or a nurse maid. But a good boss sees you as a whole person with a life apart from your work life.

You can always tell the quality of your relationship with your boss by how free you feel to speak honestly, openly, and directly to him or her about things that are bothering you. When you see your boss coming, you feel happy and comfortable rather than nervous or insecure. Perhaps the best measure of all is that when you are working with the right boss, you laugh a lot at work. You enjoy yourself and you feel valuable and important as an employee and as a person.

LOOK AT YOUR JOB OBJECTIVELY

Here is another place that you must practice zero-based thinking on a regular basis. Review your current job situation. Would you take this job, working for this boss, knowing what you now know, if you had to do it over? If the answer is no, you should seriously consider changing your position and finding a boss that you like and respect.

A friend of mine found himself working for a critical and demanding boss in a medium-size company. He liked the company. He liked the products and services that the company offered. He liked his co-workers. But his boss was making him miserable. So he looked around within the company and selected a boss who was completely different. He then arranged to transfer out of his department and into the department where he was working under the better boss. This decision changed his career completely. As a result of working under a great boss, he performed at his very best. He was paid more and promoted faster and in a few years was a manager himself.

DEVELOP A POSITIVE ATTITUDE

Fully 85 percent of your success in work, no matter how intelligent or skilled you are, is going to be determined by your attitude and your personality. Your success, how much you are paid, and how fast you are promoted will be largely determined by how much people like you and want to help you.

Well-known psychologist Dr. Daniel Goleman has written several books on the subject of emotional intelligence. His conclusion is that emotional quotient (EQ) is more important than your intelligence quotient (IQ) in determining how successful you will be at your job. Just think about it: People who are positive, cheerful, and optimistic are always more liked and valued than people who are critical, pessimistic, and negative. Positive people are the first hired and the last laid off or fired.

BE A TEAM PLAYER

One of the most important determinants of your career success will be how well you perform as a part of a team at every stage of your work. The very best team players are those who are cheerful, positive, and supportive of others. They have high levels of empathy and consideration. They are the kind of people who others want to be around and to help.

Research shows that a positive, cheerful person is more likely to be paid more and promoted faster. This kind of person is more readily noticed by supervisors who can accelerate his or her career. In addition, a positive person is supported by his or her co-workers and staff. There seems to be an upward pressure that drives a positive person forward at a faster rate.

The critical determinant of a positive mental attitude is how you function under stress. Anyone can be positive when things are going great. But it is when you face difficulties and setbacks that you show yourself, and everyone else, what you are really made of. As the saying goes: "When the going gets tough, the tough get going."

People with positive mental attitudes look for the good in every person and every situation. They look for something positive or humorous. The positive person tends to be constructive rather than destructive. And the good news is that a positive mental attitude is something that you can learn by practicing being positive, every single day, especially when it is most needed. Look for the good in each person and situation. Seek the valuable lesson in each problem or difficulty.

CREATE A POSITIVE IMAGE

It is absolutely amazing how many people hold themselves back, year after year, because no one has ever taken them aside and told them how important their external appear-ance is to getting paid more and promoted faster.

I have personally studied the subject of image in business for many years. I have read dozens of books and articles and taught thousands of people. I can tell you with great assurance that how you look on the outside is going to have a major effect on how far you go and how fast you get there.

The first rule is that you should always dress for suc-cess in your job and in your company. Look at the top peo-ple in your industry. Look at the top people in your company. Look at the pictures of the men and women in the newspapers and magazines who are being promoted to positions of higher responsibility and pay. Dress and groom the way they do. Pattern yourself after the leaders, not the followers.

There are specific colors and color combinations that are more acceptable than others in business. Buy a good book on professional image, read it from cover to cover, and then follow its recommendations in your career.

DRESS-DOWN FRIDAYS

There is a lot of talk today about casual dress. But the people who are allowed to dress casually at work are back-office people. They are not people who deal with customers. They are usually not people upon whom the future of the com-pany depends. Even in Silicon Valley, where it is a badge of honor to dress down completely, the young executives keep tailored suits in their offices, and they wear these suits when customers or investment bankers visit. They know the importance of dress.

My rule is this: If you are a person with a future, don't dress like a person without one. Dress like you are going somewhere in your life. And if everyone around you decides on casual dress, this is all the better for you. You will stand out and look better to everyone who can have a positive influence on your career.

Remember, companies want to be proud of the employees whom they introduce to their customers and their bankers. You must look like the kind of person an executive would be proud to introduce to another executive as being a representative of your company.

FIRST IMPRESSIONS ARE LASTING

The rule is this: People judge you in the first four seconds. They will then grant you approximately 30 seconds more before they make a final decision and store this judgment away in their subconscious minds. After that, it is very hard for them to change their first impressions. From then on, they will seek out evidence to prove that their first impressions were correct and will ignore evidence to the contrary. You never get a second chance to make a good first impression.

People are extremely visual. Fully 95 percent of the first impression you make will be determined by your clothes and grooming. One rule for proper dress says that you should spend *twice* as much on your clothes and buy half as many. No matter what others might say, human beings are very strongly affected by the dress and external appearance of other people. Your goal is to dress so that you look really good in every business situation.

GOOD GROOMING IS ESSENTIAL

Your grooming is very important as well. Always strive to look like a winner at work. Look like a valuable and important person. Look like you are a person with a great future who is going somewhere with the company.

One of my clients came to me, after many months of frustration in working with a sales prospect for his company, and asked for my advice. He wanted to know why he was working so hard and selling so little. I politely told him that his appearance was such that he did not come across as trustworthy or credible to his prospective customers. He was a nice guy, but he was tripping himself up by the way he appeared on the outside. He was wearing a full beard, and research shows that people with full beards come across as having something to hide. They are not trusted.

He asked me what he could do specifically to change his appearance, and I told him. "Shave off your beard," I said. He was shocked. He wrestled with his choice of facial hair. Nonetheless, he shaved off his beard completely. The following Monday, he went back to see the prospect he had been calling on for six months. The customer's response was so totally different toward him that he was amazed. After six months of going back and forth without result, the client decided to buy and gave him a deposit check for $30,000 to seal the deal that very day.

You are a wonderful person with a wonderful future in front of you. It is important that everyone who sees you recognizes this fact in the first four seconds.

START EARLIER, WORK HARDER, AND STAY LATER

Develop a *workaholic* mentality. There is nothing that will bring attention from the important people in your work life faster than for you to get a reputation as a hard, hard worker.

Everyone in the company knows who the hard workers are. The hardest workers are always the most respected in any company of value. They are always paid more and promoted faster for a very simple reason: They get more work done in a shorter period of time. They are more valuable to the company. They set a better example and they are the kind of people whom bosses are proud of and want to keep more than anyone else.

Two extra hours of work each day is all you really need to become one of the most successful people of your generation. You can get this extra two hours by coming in an hour earlier and staying one hour later. In most cases, this will expand your day slightly but it will expand your career tremendously. You can gain extra time by working through lunch rather than taking a 60- to 90-minute break in the middle of each day.

WORK ALL THE TIME YOU WORK

The top people in every field work more hours than average people. The studies show that the top 10 percent of money earners in America work 50 to 60 hours per week. In addition, they *work all the time they work*. They do not waste time. When they arrive at work early, they immediately start in on important tasks. They work steadily throughout the day. They do not make small talk or chitchat with their co-workers.

This must be your work style as well. Work all the time you work. Do not surf the Internet, make personal phone calls, read the newspaper, or chat about the latest football game or television program. Work all the time you work.

According to Robert Half International, the average person today works at less than 50 percent of capacity. The other 50 percent is spent idly socializing, making personal phone calls, conducting personal business, starting late, leaving early, and taking extended coffee breaks and lunch hours. Only about 5 percent of people in the world of work today actually work the whole time. Everyone else is functioning somewhere below his or her potential, and in many cases, far, far below.

WIN THE CONTEST

Imagine that your company is going to bring in an outside company to assess all the staff in terms of who works the hardest, all the way down to who works the least hard.

Make it your goal to win this contest even though it is just imaginary. Your job is to be ranked as the hardest-working person in the entire company within 12 months. This will help you to get paid more and promoted faster than almost anything else you can possibly do.

The average person today only works about 32 hours per week after all coffee breaks, lunches, and traveling time has been deducted. Of these 32 hours, the average working person then wastes half the time on tasks of low value, producing only an average amount of work. Wages and salaries are eventually watered down to compensate for the low level of work that is actually being done. But this is not for you. When you start work, hit the ground running. Avoid time-wasting activities, and especially, time-wasting people.

When someone tries to distract you from what you are doing, smile cheerfully and say, "Well, I've got to get back to work!" Keep repeating these words, over and over, "Back to work! Back to work! Back to work!" If people want to talk or shoot the breeze, tell them that you have to get "Back to work!" and that you would be pleased to chat with them at the end of the day. In most cases, they will go waste someone else's time and never come back.

PUSH TO THE FRONT

The unavoidable fact is that life is a *contest*. You are in competition with everyone else who wants to be paid more and promoted faster. There is a race on and you are in it. Your job is to move yourself into the pole position and move ahead faster than anyone else.

Fortunately, there are proven and tested ways for you to come out ahead. One of the most important is for you to continually ask for more responsibility. Volunteer for every assignment. Go to your boss at least once every week and ask him or her for more responsibility.

I stumbled onto this method of rapid promotion many years ago when I was working for the chairman of a large conglomerate. Every week, I would go to him and ask him for more responsibility. For the first few weeks, he responded politely but did not give me anything extra to do. Finally, he asked me if I would perform a particular task for him, "When you have a spare moment."

SEIZE THE OPPORTUNITY

This was my chance! It was Friday night and he had asked me for a complete report on a prospective investment. I immediately went to work. I worked Friday evening and all day Saturday and Sunday. On Monday morning, I came in early and got one of the secretaries to type up the report so it looked great. I was ready, well in advance.

At 10:30 that Monday morning, he called my office and asked me if there was any way that I could get him the numbers that he had requested on Friday. The bank had called and unexpectedly asked him for the details so it could make a decision. I went straight to his office with the report and put it on his desk. He looked at it, looked up at me, and then picked up the phone and called the bank. As I sat there, he concluded a major loan reading from my analysis. From that day on, my career took off. I started to get more responsibility. I became his "go-to guy," and my entire future with that company moved onto an upward trajectory.

ALWAYS DO MORE THAN YOU ARE PAID FOR

Most people in the world of work do only what is asked of them. But this is not for you. Your job is to keep asking for more work to do, and whenever you are given a new responsibility, fulfill it quickly and dependably. Develop a reputation for being the kind of person who, if you want to get something done, tackles what is given to you.

There are fewer things that will help you get paid more and promoted faster than a reputation for *speed and dependability.* Be the kind of person your boss can count on to get the job done fast. Whatever it takes, treat every assignment that you receive as if it were a test upon which your future career depended.

WATCH FOR OPPORTUNITIES TO PERFORM

A young man in a large company told me this story. It was time for the annual United Way campaign in his company but no one would volunteer to head it up. All of the other managers avoided this job because it was so time-consuming.

But the young man saw it as an opportunity to perform for senior people in the company. He leaped at the responsibility and did an outstanding job getting everyone in the company to contribute to making the campaign a success. In the course of running the campaign, he was able to meet with almost every senior manager in the company and give each a chance to get to know him.

As a result of the success of the campaign, the president of the company was given a special award and written up in the newspapers as one of the top executives in the community. Within six months after the campaign ended this young man had been promoted twice. A year later, his previous manager, who had avoided this responsibility, was working under him.

ASK FOR WHAT YOU WANT

This is one of the most important success principles you will ever learn to put your career onto the fast track. The future belongs to the *askers*. The future does not belong to those people who sit passively, wishing and hoping that their lives and their work will somehow improve. The future belongs to those people who step up and ask for what they want. And if they don't get it, they ask, again and again, until they do get it.

When you are applying for a new job and you are offered a particular salary, ask for more at the very beginning. Most bosses have a salary range in mind of 10 percent to 20 percent above what they are offering. If they like you enough to offer you a job, they are often willing to go 10 percent or 20 percent above their first offers just to get you in the first place.

Once you have a job, ask your boss what you have to do to qualify for an increase. There is no point in working really hard if you do not know exactly what it is that you have to do to get paid more and promoted faster. You have to be doing a good job on something that really matters to your boss. Go to your boss and ask, and ask again if you are still not clear.

BUILD YOUR CASE

If you want an increase, you must ask for it. And the way you ask is by building a case, as a lawyer would build a case, for the amount that you want to receive. Instead of saying that you need more money, as most people do, you use a different strategy. Put together a list of the jobs that you are currently doing and the additional experience and skills you have developed since you were hired or since your last increase. Explain the financial impact of your work on the overall operations of the company and the contribution that you are making as a top employee.

Present all this information to your boss and tell him or her that, based on all of this, you would like an increase of a specific amount of money per month and per year. In many cases, you will get the increase simply by asking for it in an intelligent way.

In some cases, you will get less than you requested. If this happens, ask what you will have to accomplish in order to get the rest of the increase that you have asked for. If your request for an increase is turned down, ask exactly what you will have to do to get the increase you requested, and exactly when that increase will be payable. Be specific. Be clear. And don't be afraid to ask.

NEVER FEAR REJECTION

The question of "asking" is a major question in human relations today. People are afraid to ask because they fear rejection. They fear being told "No." But think about it this way: Before you ask, you have nothing. If you ask and the person says no, you are in exactly the same position that you were in before. But in many cases, the person will say yes and your whole future can be different.

Sometimes people are afraid to ask because they feel that they don't deserve it. They feel that they are not good enough to be paid more than they are currently receiving. But an interesting thing happens when you begin asking for what you want. You actually begin to feel more deserving and more valuable. You begin to think in terms of *why* you are entitled to the money rather in terms of *why not*.

If you are not happy with your current job, ask to be transferred to a different job. If you are not happy with the way you are being treated, ask to be treated differently. If you are not happy with any part of your work life, ask for it to be changed.

Of course, you should ask politely. Ask courteously. Ask in a warm and friendly way. Ask cheerfully. Ask expectantly. Ask confidently. And ask persistently, if necessary. But be sure to ask. The future belongs to the askers, and the more you ask for the things you want, the more likely you are to get those things. Just try it once and you will be amazed.

OUTNEGOTIATED BY MY SECRETARY

Once I had a secretary working for me named Diane. Diane had been fired from a bank before she came to me and she very much needed a job. I was able to hire her for only $800 per month (in 1986). After two months, because she was doing such a good job, I increased her salary to $1,000 per month. And after two more months I increased her salary to $1,200 per month. This amounted to a 50 percent increase in a very short time.

After Diane had been working for me for about six months, she told me she would like to talk to me about her compensation. We arranged a time where we sat down, closed the door, and discussed her pay. She told me that she had been thinking about her salary and that she had decided that she would like an increase.

I had expected this and I told her that I was prepared to give her another $200 per month increase—to $1,400 per month. She thanked me for the thought and then told me that she had done a good deal of research in the marketplace and she had concluded that a person of her skills and abilities was worth $1,800 per month. That was the amount that she wanted.

MAKE YOURSELF MORE VALUABLE

I was surprised. I sat there looking at her and she stared back at me without blinking. Then I thought about how quickly she had learned every detail of my business. She had taken additional computer courses in the evening, on her own time, so that she could handle the bookkeeping and word processing. She had introduced herself to our customers and was handling customer service problems. She had worked on herself to become more valuable in every area.

As she sat there, I realized that she was worth the extra money. To replace her, I would have to pay as much, if not more, to someone else. I agreed to her request and gave her the increase to $1,800 per month. She thanked me with a big smile and went back to work. I just sat there shaking my head.

Here's the point. She did everything exactly right. She carefully prepared her timing and her request. Then she stepped up and asked for exactly what she wanted, giving good, solid reasons for a 50 percent increase in pay. And I paid it willingly.

For the rest of your career, you must develop the habit of asking for what you want on every occasion. Ask at the beginning of the job, ask in the middle, and ask at every stage. Ask for more responsibilities, ask for more money. Ask for more rapid advancement. But be sure to *ask*.

GUARD YOUR INTEGRITY AS A SACRED THING

Your character is your most valuable asset. It is the critical factor that others use when evaluating you for higher pay or more rapid promotion.

The key to character is *truthfulness*. No matter what, always tell the truth, in every situation. When you give your word, keep it. When you make a promise, fulfill it. When you say you'll do something, no matter what it costs, be sure to do it.

An important part of character is loyalty. Lack of loyalty is one of the biggest, most fatal mistakes that a person can make in business. When you are loyal, you never complain, condemn, or criticize your company, your boss, your products, your services, or anything else about your work. Even if you are unhappy for some reason, you keep it to yourself. You always support the people you work with, and you demonstrate complete loyalty to the person who signs your paycheck.

Shakespeare once wrote: "This above all: to thine own self be true, and it must follow, as the night the day, Thou canst not then be false to any man." Be true to yourself and then be true to everyone around you. Never compromise your integrity for anything.

The good news is that when you live with complete integrity, inside and outside, you feel wonderful about yourself. You have greater self-confidence and higher self-esteem. You feel positive and powerful. And most of all, you earn the respect, trust, and loyalty of all the people around you. Always guard your integrity as a sacred thing.

BE FUTURE-ORIENTED IN ALL YOU DO

Future-orientation, the essential attitude for leadership, requires that you develop a long-term vision for yourself and for your career. After 50 years of research, Harvard government professor Dr. Edward Banfield concluded that the most successful men and women in our society have "long time perspective." They think 10 and 20 years out into the future and they make their decisions each day based on this long time horizon. And so should you.

The most important concept in future-orientation is idealization. This requires that you idealize or imagine your ideal future career in every respect. Project yourself forward three to five years and imagine that your life was perfect and that you were doing exactly the right job for you.

Again consider the answers to these questions. If your work situation were perfect, what would it look like? What would you be doing? How much would you be earning? Who would you be working with? Where would you be working?

INCREASE YOUR CORE COMPETENCIES

Once you have idealized your perfect job, ask yourself about the kind of person you would need to become in order to get and keep that job. What kind of skills would you have? What new talents and abilities would you have to learn and develop?

Practice what is called gap analysis on your job. Look at the gap between where you are today and where you would like to be in the future. What changes should you begin making, right now, in order to fill this gap? What would you have to do to work yourself into the kind of job you want?

of the qualities of leaders in every field is that
about the future much of the time. It is important
ink about the future as well, because that is
are going to spend the rest of your life. The
nk about the future, the more optimistic and
will be. The more you develop a clear vision
want to be in the years ahead, the more likely
will take the steps each day that will make
o your reality.

out the future of your company as well.
s and trends in your business. Think about
pany is today and what your company
successful in the future. The more future-
your position, the more you will be paid
dly you will be promoted. The more fu-
are, the better decisions you will make
ve impact you will have on your com-
The more future-oriented you are, the
control of your life, your career, and
y.

r-
re
as
ol,
om
nd

and
re-
great
strat-

AL-ORIENTED IN EVERYTHING
O

ve clear, written goals and who know exactly
it in each area of their lives accomplish vastly
ple who are not sure or who are unclear about
nt.

aps nothing can help you to be paid more and
aster than for you to become an intensely goal-

oriented person. Fortunately, the skill of setting and achieving goals is something that you can learn quite quickly and then develop through practice, day after day. You can refer back to the goal-setting exercises in Chapter 3 and apply them to advancing your career.

BE RESULT-ORIENTED IN YOUR ACTIVITIES

Your ability to get results is the single most important dete minant of how much you are paid and how rapidly you a promoted. Results are everything. Study after study h found that within two years of leaving college or scho your education has little or no impact on your career. Fr that point on, all that matters is your ability to perform get results for your company.

Many people start off with limited education skills but, as the result of focusing single-mindedly or sults, they accomplish vastly more than people with educations and lots of advantages. This must be your egy as well.

SET PRIORITIES IN YOUR WORK

Here is an exercise for you: Make a list of all of you tasks and activities. Take this list to your boss and as boss to prioritize the list.

What does he or she consider to be more im or less important on your list? From that moment on work on the tasks that your boss considers to be more important than anything else.

There is no better way to get paid more and promoted faster than for you to be working, all day long, on the tasks that are of greatest concern to your boss. The best days of your working life will be when you are working on those tasks that your boss considers most important. And the good news is that, the more you accomplish important tasks, the more important tasks you will be given to accomplish.

BECOME INTENSELY SOLUTION-ORIENTED

Your life and work will be a continuous succession of problems. You will have to deal with problems all day long and into the evenings. This is your job. Whatever your title, you are a problem solver.

Where there are no problems, you are unnecessary. The work can be automated and done by a machine. And the more that minor problems or activities are automated, the more important and valuable you become in solving problems of greater complexity.

The only interruption in this continuous flow of problems will be the occasional crisis. If you are living a normal life, you will have a crisis every two or three months. Your ability to deal effectively with the inevitable and unavoidable crisis is a key measure of your intelligence, ability, and maturity.

Solution-oriented people are the most valuable people in any organization. You can change your mind from negative to positive in a single moment by taking your thoughts off of the problem and focusing them on the solution. Instead of asking or worrying about who did what and who is to blame, you should instead ask the question, "What do we do now?"

The more you focus on finding solutions, the more solutions you will find. The better you get at solving problems, the bigger the problems you will be given to solve, and the more money, power, and position you will be given to go along with the size of the problems.

Your entire career will ultimately be determined by your ability to solve the problems that you meet at your level. And when you do, you automatically get moved up to a higher level, exactly as you get moved to a higher grade in school when you have passed the exams at the previous grade.

A SIMPLE, SEVEN-STEP PROBLEM-SOLVING METHOD

Here is a method you can use for the rest of your career to deal effectively with any problem that comes along:

1. *Define the problem clearly.* What exactly has happened? Get the facts. Get the real facts. Not the apparent facts or the obvious facts, but the real, true facts of the situation. It is amazing how much time and energy are wasted attempting to solve a problem when the people involved are not even clear on what the problem is in the first place. Keep asking, "What else is the problem?"

2. *Identify all the possible causes of this problem.* How and why did it happen? Sometimes this exercise alone will point to the correct solution.

3. *Identify all the possible solutions.* The more possible solutions you can come up with, the more likely it is that you will come up with the ideal one. Keep asking, "What else is the solution?"

4. *Make a decision to implement one of the solutions.* In most cases, any decision is usually better than no decision at all. A poor decision vigorously enacted is better than a brilliant decision that sits on the shelf.

5. *Assign responsibility for carrying out the decision.* Who exactly is going to do what, and when, and to what standard?

6. *Set a schedule of reporting and a standard to measure whether the decision has been successful.* A solution without a deadline or a standard is really not a solution at all.

7. *Take immediate action.* Implement the solution, or have it implemented, and resolve the problem.

Become solution-oriented in your approach toward life and work. Become the kind of person to whom people bring their problems because you always have a solution. The more you focus on solutions, the smarter you become. The more solution-oriented you become, the more and better solutions you will come up with. You can put your entire life and career on the fast track toward being paid more and promoted faster by becoming an intensely solution-oriented person.

BECOME IDEA-ORIENTED IN YOUR JOB

Being idea-oriented means continually looking for faster, better, cheaper, easier ways to get the job done and to get the desired result.

The good news is this: You are a genius! You have more natural intelligence and creativity than you have ever used in your entire life. But your creativity is like a muscle: If you don't use it, you lose it. And the more you use your mental ability to generate ideas, the smarter you become, and the more and better ideas you generate to use in every part of your work.

The most successful people in every business are those people who are always coming up with new and better ideas, new and better ways to achieve the goals of the company. And no one is smarter than you. No one is better than you. No one has more natural creativity than you have, just as no one has more or different muscles than you. It is all a matter of how often and how long you use your creative muscles in your life and your work.

PRACTICE MINDSTORMING ON PROBLEMS

Here is one of the greatest idea-generating methods ever discovered. More people have become successful with this method than any other creative-thinking method in America. It is called mindstorming.

In mindstorming, you take your major problem or goal and you write it in the form of a question at the top of a page. You then generate 20 answers or more to this question. For example, your question could be, "How can we reduce the time and costs of this activity by 20 percent?" Then, alone or with others, you develop 20 answers to that question. At the end of this exercise, you select at least one of the answers and take action on it immediately.

For the rest of your career, whenever you have a big challenge, problem, or goal, write it as a question at the top of the page and then discipline yourself to generate at least 20 answers to your question. This single exercise alone will change your life. It will dramatically increase your intelligence. It will activate your creativity so that it runs all day long. It will actually make you smarter and increase your IQ. By practicing mindstorming on a regular basis, you make your mind stronger, faster, and more flexible than ever before. Just try it once. You will be amazed.

The more ideas you come up with to improve the operations of your business, the more you will be paid and the faster you will be promoted.

BECOME PEOPLE-ORIENTED IN YOUR JOB

Relationships are everything. Your level of success, your rate of promotion, and your pay will be largely determined by the number of people you know and who know you in a positive way.

Birds of a feather flock together. People like to pay and promote people who they like and feel comfortable with. The more people like you and enjoy your company, the more doors they will open for you and the more obstacles they will remove from your path.

A recent study found that companies were much more likely to lay off people with negative personalities even though those people might have been technically superior to others. In a 20-year study of hiring and firing trends, fully 95 percent of people who were let go by their companies were let go because of personality problems. Poor social skills are the number-one obstacle to getting paid more and promoted faster.

PRACTICE THE GOLDEN RULE

The key to becoming a people-oriented person is for you to practice the golden rule in everything you do. Treat other people the way you would like them to treat you. Offer to help other people to do their jobs whenever you see an opportunity. Practice being courteous, kind, and considerate when you deal with other people, especially people who work in lesser-paid positions than your own. Thomas Carlyle once wrote, "You can tell a big person by the way he treats little people."

Continually expand your network of contacts in every way possible. Join your local business associations and attend every business function related to your field. Introduce yourself to other people and find out what they do. Ask good questions and listen carefully to the answers.

Make your network of contacts wider and wider so that you are eventually known to a great number of the key people in your industry.

GET TO KNOW THE KEY PEOPLE

Many people have transformed their careers by getting to know other key people in their industry. As a result, when positions came open, they were remembered, offered interviews, and eventually the jobs. Many people have gone from doing a good job at one place to becoming a senior executive with higher pay and stock options at another place just because of a contact or friendship that developed at a business or association meeting.

In your work, become a friendly, helpful, and cheerful person. Express gratitude to people on every occasion. Say thank you to anyone who does anything for you, either large or small. Go out of your way to compliment people on their traits, possessions, or accomplishments. As Abraham Lincoln said, "Everyone likes a compliment."

Treat each person in your company as if he or she were one of the most valuable customers of the business. Treat your boss, your co-workers, and your staff as if they were all valuable and important people. When you make other people feel important, they will look for every opportunity to make you feel important as well. And when you are liked and respected by all the people around you, all kinds of opportunities will open up for you to be paid more and promoted faster.

BECOME GROWTH-ORIENTED IN YOUR CAREER

Dedicate yourself to lifelong learning. Set yourself apart from the crowd by being the person in the company who is learning and growing at a faster rate than anyone else.

The fact is that most of your knowledge and skill today has a half-life of about two and a half years. This means that within five years most of what you know today about your field will be obsolete or irrelevant. In order to survive and thrive in a fast-changing world, you will have to continually upgrade your knowledge and skills, at a faster and faster rate, just to stay even, much less get ahead.

The highest paid 10 percent of Americans read two to three hours each day in their fields just to keep current. They are continually taking in information from every possible source. As we move at hyperspeed into the information age, the top people in every business realize that they must stay ahead of the wave of change or they will be bowled over by it. Today, you have a very simple choice. You can be a master of change or you can be a victim of change. There is very little middle ground. Your job is to be a master of change by continually learning to be better and better at what you do.

THREE KEYS TO LIFELONG LEARNING

The first is for you to *read* at least one hour each day in your chosen field. Reading is to the mind as exercise is to the body. If you read a good book on your field for one hour each day, that will translate into about one book per week. One book per week will translate into roughly 50 books per year. Fifty books per year will translate into 500 books over the next 10 years. The very act of continuously reading in your field will make you one of the most knowledgeable and highest-paid people in your business in a very short time.

The second key to continuous learning is for you to *listen* to audio programs in your car as you drive from place to place. The average car owner sits behind the wheel 500 to 1,000 hours each year. That is the equivalent of three to six months of 40-hour weeks that you spend in your car, or one to two full-time university semesters, according to the University of Southern California. You can become one of the most knowledgeable people in your field by listening to educational audio programs rather than music in your car.

The third key to continuous learning is for you to *take every good course and seminar in your field* that you can find. The highest-paid people I know will actually travel from one side of the country to the other in order to take an intense two- or three-day seminar that can help them in their careers. A good book, audio program, or seminar can give you ideas and insights that can save you years of hard work, as can good Internet research. From now on, become greedy for new knowledge. In the final analysis, nothing can help you to get paid more and promoted faster than becoming one of the most knowledgeable and competent people in your field.

BECOME EXCELLENCE-ORIENTED IN EVERYTHING YOU DO

Resolve to be the best at what you do. Resolve today to join the top 10 percent of people in your field. Look around you at the top people and realize that no one is smarter than you and no one is better than you. If people are ahead of you today, it is because they are doing things differently from you. And whatever anyone else has done, you can do as well, if you just learn how.

The way that you become one of the best people in your field is for you to, first of all, identify your key result areas. These are the skill areas where you absolutely, positively have to do an excellent job in order to be successful in your field. There are seldom more than five to seven key result areas in any job. Your ability to perform at an excellent level in each of these areas is the key determinant of how much you are paid and how fast you are promoted.

Once you have identified your key result areas, ask yourself this key question: "What one skill, if I developed and practiced it in an excellent fashion, would have the greatest positive impact on my career?" This is the most important question you will ever ask and answer for your career. If you do not know which one skill can help you the most, go to your boss and ask him or her. Ask your co-workers. Ask your spouse. But whatever it takes, you absolutely must find out the answer to this question and center in on the one key skill that can help you the very most if you master it at a high level. Then, set the acquisition of this skill as a goal. Write it down. Make a plan to master this skill. You then work on it every single day. This simple exercise is so powerful that it alone can change your life.

Set standards of excellent performance for yourself in everything you do. Develop a reputation for quality work. If you are a manager or supervisor, demand quality work from everyone who reports to you. Remember the old saying, "Good enough seldom is."

In the final analysis, no one will care how fast you did the job. All people will care about is how *well* you did the job. Resolve to become absolutely excellent at what you do, and do your job in an excellent fashion. Set this as your standard and never compromise it for the rest of your career.

BECOME CUSTOMER-ORIENTED IN YOUR BUSINESS

In business, customers are everything. The essential purpose of a business is to create and keep customers. Profits in a business are the result of creating and keeping customers in a sufficient number and at a reasonable cost.

Customers pay all salaries and wages. Customers determine the success or failure of companies and of everyone in the company. Sam Walton once said, "There is only one boss—the customer—and he or she can fire everybody in the company from the chairman down, simply by spending his or her money elsewhere."

The definition of a customer is someone who depends on you for the satisfaction of their needs, or someone who you depend upon for the satisfaction of your needs. By this definition, your boss is your customer. Your co-workers are your customers. Your staff members are your customers.

And of course, the people who buy your products and services are your customers. Everyone is dependent on someone else for something. Who are your customers? Who are your key customers?

Your success in your life and your career will be largely determined by how well you serve and satisfy the customers in your life. And the more and the better you satisfy your customers, the more customers you will be given to satisfy.

FOUR LEVELS OF CUSTOMER SATISFACTION

There are four levels of customer satisfaction in your business. The first is to *meet* customer expectations. This is the minimum for survival.

The second level is for you to *exceed* customer expectations, for you to do more than the customer expected. This is the key to growth and profitability.

The third level of customer satisfaction is for you to *delight* your customers, to do something that causes them to light up with unexpected pleasure.

The highest level of customer satisfaction is where you *amaze* your customers, where you do things that make them so happy that they not only want to buy from you again, but they want to bring their friends as well.

Every single day, you should be looking for ways to exceed expectations and both amaze and delight the people

who depend upon you at work. Your ability to serve and satisfy your customers will get you paid more and promoted faster than anything else you can do.

BECOME PROFIT-ORIENTED IN YOUR BUSINESS

This is the key to your financial future. This is the key to growth, success, and rapid promotion. The most important people in every organization are intensely focused on what they can do to increase the profitability of the company. And the greater effect your work can have on profitability, the more important you are and the more you will be paid

There are two ways to increase profitability in a c
pany:

- Increase revenues by selling more of the products and services or by developing ucts and services that can be sold to mo

- Decrease the costs of providing the p vices to the existing market, thereb margins.

The best combination is fo looking for ways to increase sale ducing the costs of delivering th

Fully 80 percent of a market in five years do not and change is extraordin for new products and

Power is
and busin
your caree
explain.

existing products and services, that you can bring to the market to maintain and increase revenues for your organization. One good idea is all you need to change your entire career.

At the same time, you should be looking for ways to reorganize, restructure, and reengineer every part of your work so that you can get the job done faster and at a lower cost than before. Squeeze out every extra penny of expense. Examine every single cost to see if it cannot be decreased, downsized, or eliminated in some way. Many executives have found that they can cut the cost of producing a product or service by 50 percent, 60 percent, and 70 percent while increasing the speed at which that product or service is brought to the market. And so can you.

The key people in any organization are those who are the most concerned with the overall profitability of the company. And when you become a key player in affecting profitability in some way, you come immediately to the attention of the key people who can most help you in your career. Your ability to increase profitability in some way is one of the very fastest ways for you to get paid more and promoted faster.

BECOME POWER-ORIENTED IN YOUR RELATIONSHIPS WITH OTHERS

a very real and important part of organizational ess life. Your ability to acquire and use power in is essential to your long-term success. Let me

Power, in its simplest sense, means control over people and resources. Power means that you have the ability to influence things that are done or that are not done. There are two major forms of power: positive power and negative power. Positive power is where you use your influence to help the organization achieve more of its goals, faster and cheaper. Negative power is where people use their positions or influence to improve themselves at the expense of the organization.

There are three forms of positive power that you should develop. The first is called *expert power*. Expert power arises when you become very good at doing something that is important to the company. As a result, people look up to you and respect you for the value of the contribution you can make.

The second form of power is called *ascribed power*. This is where you are liked and admired by others because of your ability to be a team player, to get along with others, and to help others to achieve their goals and do their jobs. Ascribed power arises when people like you and want you to be successful. This comes from your attitude and your personality more than anything else.

The third kind of power is *position power*. This is the power, authority, and ability to reward and punish that goes along with a specific title. Every title or position has some of this power attached to it. As you develop expert power and ascribed power, you will be given position power. The people above you and around you will want you to be in a position of influence because you have demonstrated that the more influence you have, the more and better results you can get for the company. This is the very best and most important of all powers for you to develop and build.

And the more you acquire and use your power in a positive and constructive way, the more power you will attract to you. More people around you will support you and help you. The people above you will give you more resources. You will be more respected and esteemed by others. And you will definitely be paid more and promoted faster.

BECOME ACTION-ORIENTED IN YOUR CAREER

Action orientation is the most outwardly identifiable quality of a high performer. He is constantly in motion. He is always doing something that is moving himself and the company toward the achievement of its goals.

Resolve today to develop a sense of urgency. Develop a bias for action. Develop a fast tempo in everything you do, because the faster you move, the more you get done. And the more you get done, the more experience you get and the more competent you become. The faster you move, the more energy you have. The faster you move, the more valuable you become to your company and to everyone around you.

Only 2 percent of people in our society have a sense of urgency. And these are the people who eventually rise to the top of every organization. When you develop a reputation for speed and dependability in everything you do, you attract to yourself more opportunities to do more things of greater and greater importance.

An average person with an average background who moves fast and continuously will eventually run circles around a genius who moves slowly and carefully. Your goal is to develop the reputation for being the person who, if somebody wants a job done fast, is trusted with the task. This will open more doors for you and get you paid more and promoted faster than almost anything you can possibly do.

Today, the primary source of wealth is talent and ability. All the money and resources flows to the men and women who demonstrate that they can get the job done and get it done quickly and well. When you begin to practice these techniques to get paid more and promoted faster, you will put your career onto the fast track. You will move ahead more rapidly and more dependably than anyone else around you. You will move upward and onward, and you will make your life and career into something truly extraordinary.

QUESTIONS FOR REFLECTION

1. Imagine that everyone in your company was going to be rated in terms of who worked the hardest. How would you score?

2. What steps could you start taking on a daily basis to upgrade your knowledge and skills?

3. Which of your tasks contribute the greatest value to your company?

4. What are your boss's most important concerns and priorities?

5. Who are the major time wasters in your office and how could you avoid them?

6. What are the types of tasks that need to be done quickly and well in your company?

7. What one action are you going to take immediately as the result of what you have learned in this chapter?

7

How Do You Get the Most out of Yourself?

*"*If one advances confidently in the direction of his dreams, and endeavors to live the life which he has imagined, he will meet with a success unexpected in common hours.*"*
—HENRY DAVID THOREAU

WHAT YOU ARE ABOUT TO LEARN in this final chapter on reinvention can change your life. These ideas, methods, and techniques can increase your efficiency and effectiveness, boost your productivity, double your income, lower your stress levels, and make you one of the most productive people in your business or field today.

All successful people are very productive. They work longer hours and they put more into each hour. They get a lot more done than the average person. They get paid more and promoted faster. They are highly respected and esteemed by everyone around them. They become leaders and role models. Inevitably, they rise to the top of their fields and to the highest income levels, and so can you.

Each of these tested and proven strategies for managing your time and doubling your productivity is learnable through practice and repetition. Each of these methods, when you practice them regularly, will eventually become habits of both thinking and working.

When you begin applying these techniques to your work and to your life, your self-esteem, self-confidence, self-respect, and sense of personal pride will increase immediately. The payoff for you will be tremendous, for the rest of your life.

MAKE A DECISION!

Every positive change in your life begins with a clear, unequivocal decision that you are going to either do something or stop doing something. Significant change starts when you decide to either get in or get out, to either fish or cut bait.

Decisiveness is one of the most important qualities of successful and happy men and women, and decisiveness is developed through practice and repetition, over and over again, until it becomes as natural to you as breathing in and breathing out.

The sad fact is that many people are poor because they have not yet decided to be rich. People are overweight and unfit because they have not yet decided to be thin and trim. People are inefficient and unproductive because they haven't yet decided to be well organized and highly productive.

MAKE A FIRM RESOLUTION

Decide today that you are going to become an expert in time management and personal productivity, no matter how long it takes or how much you invest to achieve it. Resolve today that you are going to practice these principles, over and over again, until they become second nature.

Discipline yourself to do what you know you need to do to be the very best in your field. Perhaps the best definition of self-discipline comes from philosopher and writer Elbert Hubbard: "Self-discipline is the ability to make yourself do what you should do, when you should do it, whether you feel like it or not."

It is easy to do something when you feel like it. It's when you don't feel like it and you force yourself to do it anyway that you move your life and career onto the fast track.

What decisions do you need to make today in order to start moving toward the top of your field? Whatever it is, to get in or get out, make a decision today and then get started. This single act alone can change the whole direction of your life.

SET CLEAR GOALS AND OBJECTIVES

Perhaps the most important word on the road to success is *clarity*. Fully 80 percent of your success comes from being absolutely clear about what it is you are trying to accomplish. Unfortunately, probably 80 percent or more of failure and frustration is because people are vague or fuzzy about what it is they want and how to go about achieving it.

The great oil billionaire H. L. Hunt once said that there are only two real requirements for great success. First, he said, "Decide exactly what it is you want." Most people never do this. Second, he said, "You must determine the price you are going to have to pay to get it and then resolve to pay that price."

You can have just about anything you really want as long as you are willing to pay the price. And nature always demands that you pay the price in full, and in advance.

PLAN EVERY DAY IN ADVANCE

Daily planning is absolutely essential if you want to increase your productivity. Practice the "six P" formula for high achievement: proper prior planning prevents poor performance.

Proper planning is the mark of the professional. All successful men and women take a good deal of time to plan their activities. The 10/90 Rule says that the first 10 percent of time that you spend planning your activities will save you as much as 90 percent of the time necessary to perform those activities once you start work.

Always think on paper. Something wonderful happens between your head and your hand when you write out your plans in detail. Writing actually sharpens your thinking, stimulates your creativity, and enables you to focus far better than just thinking about it in your mind.

Begin the planning process by making a master list of everything you can think of that you have to do for the long-term future. This master list then becomes the central control list for your life. Whenever you think of something new that you have to do, write it down on this master list.

At the beginning of each month, make a monthly list covering everything that you can think of that you will have to do in the coming weeks. Then, break your monthly list down into weekly lists and specify exactly when you are going to start and complete the tasks that you have decided upon for your month. Finally, and perhaps most important, make a daily list of your activities, preferably the night before, so that your subconscious mind can work on your list while you sleep.

Always work from a list. When something new comes up during the day, write it down on your list before you do it. As you work, tick off each item as you complete it. This gives you an ongoing sense of accomplishment and personal progress. Crossing off items one by one motivates and energizes you. A list serves as a scorecard to chart your day. It shows you that you are making progress and makes clear what you still have to do.

According to time-management experts, Alan Lakein among them, working from a list will increase your productivity by 25 percent from the very first day you begin doing it. Most highly effective people think on paper and work from written lists.

PLAN EVERY PROJECT CAREFULLY

Virtually everything that you do today is a project of some kind. A project is defined as a multitask activity. It is a job that takes several steps to complete. In this sense, you are a project manager throughout your career.

Your success in life, your pay, and your promotability are largely determined by your ability to complete projects or multitask jobs. And fortunately, you can become an expert in this area with a few simple instructions. As in other areas of time management, the most important word is *clarity.*

There are six things to remember.

1. Start each project with a clear definition of the ideal finished result, as if it were perfect in every respect.

2. Make a list of every step in the project—every little thing that has to be done to get from the beginning to the end of the completed task.

3. Organize the list by priority and sequence. What has to be done first? What has to be done second? What activities can be done simultaneously?

4. Assign responsibility for each part of the project. Decide exactly who is to do what and by when. A project plan without assigned responsibilities and specific deadlines is merely a business conversation. It doesn't lead to a specific result.

5. Monitor the project closely, especially if it is important and can have significant consequences. Make sure everything is on track. Develop a reputation for

getting your large jobs done on schedule or well before schedule.

6. Inspect what you expect. Never trust luck. Never assume that all will be well. Always ask, "What could possibly go wrong?" and, "Of all the things that could go wrong, what's the worst possible thing that could go wrong?" And then make sure that it doesn't happen.

Look at the project and ask, "What is the key element or most vital part of this project? What could interfere with that key element being done on time?" Remember that proper prior planning prevents poor performance. Your ability to plan each step of your projects carefully and thoroughly can dramatically increase your productivity and your results.

USE THE ABCDE METHOD TO SET PRIORITIES

This is one of the most powerful time-management techniques for setting priorities and getting organized. The beauty of this method lies in the fact that it is so simple and easy to use and apply.

The key to increasing your productivity and your value, in any area of your work or at any time of your life, is for you to select your most important task and then for you to discipline yourself to work on that task until it is complete. All of time management revolves around helping you clarify, in your own mind, the most important thing you could possibly be doing, before you start.

The way that you determine your highest priority at any moment is to think about the potential *consequences* of doing or not doing a particular task. A task that is important is something that can have major consequences if it is done or not done. All highly productive people think continually about possible consequences as they plan and organize their activities.

BEGIN WITH YOUR LIST

With the ABCDE Method, you start by making a list of everything that you have to do before you begin. You then go through the list carefully and put the letter *A, B, C, D,* or *E* next to each of the five items on the list. Each of the five letters has a different meaning.

1. *An A item is something that is very important.* This is a task that you *must do,* something that has serious consequences for either doing it or not doing it. Put an *A* next to the top tasks on your list.

2. *A B item is something that you should do but it is not as important as an A item.* There are only mild consequences associated with doing it or not doing it. Returning a phone call or checking your e-mail would fall into this category. Put a *B* next to these items on your list.

3. *A C item is something that would be nice to do, but for which there are no consequences at all.* Phoning a friend, going for coffee, or chatting with a co-worker are all things that are nice to do but they have absolutely no consequences for your career or your success.

The rule is that you should never do a *B* item when there is an *A* item left undone. You should never do a *C* item when there is a *B* item left undone. You must be very disciplined about this.

4. *A* D *item is an item that you delegate or outsource to someone else.* The rule is that you should delegate everything that you possibly can to free up more time for you to concentrate on your *A* activities.

5. *The letter* E *stands for eliminate.* These are items that are of such low value that you could eliminate them completely and they would make no difference to your success at your job.

The discipline of eliminating low-value tasks can simplify your life and free up more time for you to accomplish those tasks that can have the greatest possible consequences for you.

Once you have applied the ABCDE formula to your list, go back over the list and organize your *A* tasks by priority. Put an A-1 next to your most important task, an A-2 next to your second most important task, and so on. Then, begin immediately on your A-1 task and discipline yourself to stay at it until it is finished. This simple ABCDE Method alone will double your productivity.

SEPARATE THE URGENT FROM THE IMPORTANT

Everything that you have to do during the day can be separated into one of four categories. These categories are determined by designating tasks as either urgent or not urgent, and important or not important.

The first type of task is both *urgent and important*. This is something that you have to do immediately. It is a job that is "in your face." Urgent and important tasks, like important telephone calls, meetings, customer visits, and emergencies, are almost always determined by other people. But they are vital requirements of your job. You cannot put them off without causing serious problems. Most people spend all day long doing things that are both urgent and important.

The second type of tasks are those that are *important but not urgent*. These are the items that usually have the greatest possible long-term consequences. These include preparing proposals and reports, upgrading your knowledge and skills, physical fitness and exercise, and spending time with your family.

An item that is important but not urgent is an item that can be put off until later. But it is also the kind of activity that can have a major long-term impact on your life. Tasks and activities that are not urgent but important sooner or later become very urgent indeed, like a term paper in college or a report for your boss or one of your clients.

The third category of tasks includes those items that are *urgent but not important*. These may consist of telephone calls, checking your e-mail every few minutes, co-workers dropping in to see you, casual conversations about what was on television, and so on. You may engage in these activities at work, but they have no effect on your success. Many people delude themselves into thinking that they are actually working when they are doing things that are urgent but unimportant. This, however, is a great time waster and a killer of careers and potential.

The greatest time wasters of all are those activities that are *neither urgent nor important.* These are completely useless activities. These are things that you do during the day that are completely irrelevant and have no consequences at all, like reading the newspaper, calling home to see what's for dinner, or going shopping. They contribute nothing to your company or to your personal goals.

The key to increasing your productivity is to focus on clearing up all tasks that are urgent and important—daily tasks that must be done immediately. Then begin working on those activities that are urgent but not important at the moment. You must refuse to do things that are not urgent or important at all, so you can have more time to do the things that can really make a difference.

Always ask yourself, "What are the potential consequences of doing this task? What would happen if I did not do it at all?" And whatever your answer, let it guide you in your choice of priorities.

PRACTICE THE LAW OF FORCED EFFICIENCY

This law says: There is never enough time to do everything, but there is always enough time to do the most important things. Whenever you are put under pressure to complete an important task, a task for which there are significant consequences, you put your head down and somehow get the job done by the deadline. You are forced to become efficient.

Many people cannot discipline themselves to get a job done well in advance of a deadline. They then say that they work best under pressure. However, no one works best under pressure. This is just a justification for poor time management. When you are under pressure, you not only experience more stress but you also make more mistakes. These mistakes often require that the job be redone again at a later time.

There are four excellent questions that you can ask to increase your efficiency and your productivity.

1. *"What are my highest value-added tasks?"* What is it that you do that contributes the greatest value to your work and to your life? What is it that you do that pays the very most or yields the highest rewards to you and your company? Talk to your boss and to the people around you. Ask for input. You must be absolutely clear about the answer to this question and work on these high-value activities all the time.

2. *"Why am I on the payroll?"* Exactly what have you been hired to do? And of all the things that you have been hired to do, what are the few results that most determine your success in your job? Whatever the answer to this question, these are the activities that you need to focus on all day long.

3. *"What can I and only I do that, if done well, can make a real difference?"* At any given time, there is only one answer to this question. This is the sort of task that, if you don't do it, it doesn't get done. But if you do it and you do it well, it can make a major difference. Whatever it is, you should be working on

it above all else. This is where you can make your greatest contribution.

4. *"What is the most valuable use of my time, right now?"* Whatever your answer is to that question, be sure that that is what you are doing at the moment.

Your ability to ask and answer these questions on an hourly basis will keep you focused on your top priorities and performing at your best. Disciplining yourself to work only on the tasks that are your answers to these questions can double your productivity. What is the most valuable use of your time?

APPLY THE 80/20 RULE

The 80/20 Rule, the Pareto principle, is one of the most important and powerful of all time-management principles. This rule divides all activities into what Pareto called "the vital few" and "the trivial many." This law says that 20 percent of the things you do, the vital few, will account for fully 80 percent of the value of everything you do.

The reverse of this principle is that 80 percent of the things you do will account for only 20 percent of the value of your activities. This 80/20 Rule applies to all aspects of business and personal life. In business, 80 percent of your sales will come from 20 percent of your customers. Eighty percent of your profits will come from 20 percent of your products. Eighty percent of your sales will come from 20 percent of your salespeople. Eighty percent of your income, success, and advancement will come from 20 percent of your activities.

If you make a list of ten things that you have to do in a particular day, two of those items will turn out to be worth more than all the others put together. Your ability to identify and focus on the top 20 percent of tasks will determine your success and productivity as much as any other factor.

Practice *creative procrastination* with the 80/20 Rule. Because you can't do everything, you have to procrastinate on something. Therefore, discipline yourself to procrastinate on the 80 percent of activities that contribute very little value to your life and your results.

The average person procrastinates on high-value tasks, but this is not for you. You must hold your own feet to the fire and procrastinate deliberately and continuously on those low-value items that have very few consequences if they are done or not. Before you start work, always check to make sure that what you are doing is in the top 20 percent of all the things you could be doing. Procrastinate on the rest.

WORK AT YOUR ENERGY PEAKS

One of the most important requirements for high productivity is high levels of physical, mental, and emotional energy. All highly productive, highly successful, highly paid people have high levels of energy, sustained over long periods of time.

To generate and maintain high levels of energy, you need to practice proper eating, proper exercise, and proper rest. You need to eat light, nutritious, high-protein foods and avoid fats, sugars, white flour products, pasta, potatoes, candy, soft drinks, and desserts of all kinds.

You need to get regular exercise, three to five days per week, 30 to 60 minutes each day, even if you just go for walks before or after work. I have always been amazed to find that marathoners and triathletes, people who sometimes train several hours a day, are often among the highest-paid and most productive people in their fields. There seems to be a direct relationship between physical fitness and energy on the one hand and high levels of productivity on the other.

Especially, be sure to get lots of rest, especially if you are working hard. You need at least seven or eight hours of sleep per night, and sometimes even more. You need to take at least one full day off each week and two full weeks off each year if you want to perform at your best.

You should identify the times of day that you are the brightest and most alert. For some people, this is the morning. For others it is the afternoon or evening. Whatever it is for you, you should schedule your most creative and demanding tasks during the time of day at which you are at your very best. In particular, you should do creative work, such as writing reports and proposals, at your energy peaks.

Perhaps your most valuable asset in your work is your ability to think well and perform efficiently. Maximum performance and productivity requires that you take excellent care of your physical and mental health and that you work at your most important jobs when you experience your highest levels of energy. This is a major key to high output and great success.

PRACTICE SINGLE-HANDLING WITH KEY TASKS

Single-handling is one of the most powerful of all time-management techniques. This technique alone will boost your productivity by 50 percent or more the very first day you begin practicing it. When you make single-handling a habit, you can double your productivity even if you do nothing else recommended in this chapter.

The way it works is simple. Make a list of everything you have to do. Select the most important item on your list, the highest-value use of your time. Then, start work on that most important task and discipline yourself to stay at it until it is 100 percent complete. Andrew Carnegie, who started as a day laborer in a Pittsburgh steel plant, and who became one of the richest men in the world, attributed much of his wealth and success to this simple rule. He said that it transformed his life and the lives of everyone who ever worked for him.

Remember, two of the most important qualities for success are *focus and concentration*. Focus requires the ability to be absolutely clear about your goals and priorities. Concentration requires the ability to work single-mindedly, without diversion or distraction, on one thing—the most important thing—and stay with it until it is complete. This habit, once developed, will contribute more to your success than any other habit you can develop.

STARTING AND STOPPING

The fact is that when you start a task, then put it aside, then come back to it later and start again several times, you can eventually increase the amount of time required to complete that task by as much as 500 percent.

With single-handling, however, if you begin a task and then you discipline yourself to stay at it until it is complete, you can get it done in as little as 20 percent of the time of another person. This is one of the great secrets of time management and high productivity. And it is a habit that you can learn by repetition and practice, over and over again.

There are two payoffs from single handling. The first is that you will quickly become one of the most valuable and highest-paid people in your field. The second, and even more important, is that every time you complete a major task you get an endorphin rush. Your brain releases a chemical that gives you a feeling of well-being. You feel happy and energized, and your self-esteem goes up. You feel motivated and eager to start another task. Single-handling is one of the most important of all success principles ever discovered.

EAT THAT FROG

There is an old saying that "if the very first thing you do each morning is to get up and eat a live frog, you can have the satisfaction of knowing that that is probably the worst thing that is going to happen to you all day long." There is a corollary: "If you have to eat a live frog, it doesn't pay to sit and look at it for very long." Your "frog" is the biggest, ugliest, hardest, and most challenging but most important task that you have to do at any given time or on any given day.

The jobs that can make the greatest difference in your career and in your life are invariably big, hard jobs.

These are the very jobs on which you are most likely to procrastinate. These are the jobs that you keep putting off even
though you know how important they are, or can be, if you
get them done.

Here is the formula for "eating your frog." Make a
list of everything that you have to do the next day. Organize
the list by priority, using the ABCDE Method. Select your
A-1 task, the most important thing you have to do tomorrow,
and put it in the center of your desk or workplace before
you quit for the day. Then, first thing in the morning, before
you check your e-mail, make any phone calls, read the
newspaper, or talk with your co-workers, discipline yourself to start work on that task and stay with it until it is done.
Discipline yourself to "eat your frog" every morning until it
becomes a habit.

DO THE WORST FIRST

Completing an important task first thing in the morning
starts your day with a surge of energy. From that moment
on, you will have greater focus and you will work at a higher
tempo. You will always get far more done on the day when
you "eat your frog" first thing.

About five years ago, I was conducting a strategic
planning session with a $30 million company. During the
program, to make a point, I told them the story about eating
the frog first thing in the morning. They liked the story so
much that for Christmas, every executive in the company
received a brass frog to put in the center of their desks and
remind them of the importance of this principle.

Within five years, the company's annual sales jumped from $30 million to over $100 million. And throughout the company, the executives that I continue to work with proudly point out the brass frogs on their desks and tell me what a difference it has made in their lives. Try it for yourself.

ORGANIZE YOUR WORKSPACE

Highly productive people work from a clean desk and a clean workspace. Inefficient, unproductive, confused people look the part. Their workplaces often look as though a grenade has gone off, scattering papers and files everywhere. This is not for you.

Make it a habit to clean off your workspace and to work from a clean desk all the time. Even if you have to take everything off your desk and put it behind you on the floor or on a credenza. Keep your desk clean!

Fully 30 percent of working time today is spent looking for something that has been misplaced in some way. When people say that they work better from a messy desk, it turns out not to be true at all. When these same people are forced to clean up their workspace and work on one item at a time, their productivity doubles within 24 hours. It amazes them to learn the truth.

THE TRAF FORMULA

Use what is called the TRAF formula on all your papers. The four letters stand for toss, refer, action, and file.

1. *Toss.* Your wastebasket is one of the most helpful time-management tools in your office. Throw away and toss everything that you possibly can before getting bogged down reading through it. This is especially true with direct mail advertising, unnecessary subscriptions for magazines, newspapers, or any other material that you don't need.

Today, with the Internet, this can be expanded to "delete." Use your delete button generously on everything and anything that does not need your direct attention. Refrain from reading things out of curiosity.

2. *Refer.* This is a task that someone else should deal with. Make a note on it and send it off. Take every opportunity to delegate everything you possibly can so that you have more time to do those things that only you can do.

3. *Act.* Use a red file for this purpose to make it stand out. Your action file should contain everything that you have to take action on in the foreseeable future. By putting things in your action file, you deal with them and get them out of the way.

4. *File.* These are papers and documents that you will need at a later time. But remember, before you file or store anything, fully 80 percent of all items that are filed are never looked at again. When you make a note to file something, you are creating work for someone else. Be sure that it is necessary before you file it.

WHEN IN DOUBT, THROW IT OUT

There are time-management specialists today who charge several hundred dollars to help executives clear up their desks and their offices. One of the first things these experts do is to help their clients go through the piles of material that the executive has been saving up to read at a later time. Here is the rule: If you have not read it within six months, it's junk! Throw it away.

My motto for keeping my office clean is: "When in doubt, throw it out!" This also applies to old clothes, old furniture, old toys, and anything else that is cluttering up your life in any area. Many people are pack rats in their attitude toward saving magazines, newsletters, newspapers, and other information that comes in the door. This inability to throw things out is usually a throwback from a poor childhood or from a parent who had a poor childhood.

The fact is that you will never be able to read all the information you receive on a daily basis. You must discipline yourself to throw it away as quickly as you possibly can. Keep your workspace clean and keep only one thing in front of you at a time. This will dramatically increase your productivity.

USE TRAVEL TIME PRODUCTIVELY

The two major forms of travel time today are driving and flying. You should turn both of these forms of transition time into productive work or learning time.

When you drive, always listen to educational audio programs. The average person sits in a car 500 to 1,000 hours each year. This is the equivalent of one to two full-time university semesters. Experts at the University of Southern California recently concluded that you can get the same benefit as full-time university attendance by simply listening to educational audio programs as you drive from place to place. Turn your car into a university on wheels. View your car as a learning machine for the rest of your career.

Many people have become highly educated and moved to the tops of their fields with audio learning. You should do the same. You should resolve from this day forward that your car will never be moving without something educational playing.

YOUR OFFICE IN THE SKY

When you are flying, you should use this time productively as well. Time-management experts have found that every hour of work in an airplane is equal to three hours of work in a busy office. The reason for this is you can work without any interruptions at all on an airplane, if you plan it and organize it in advance.

Look upon every flight as an opportunity to work and increase your productivity. Plan your trip. Prepare a work schedule. Write up an agenda for the things that you are going to accomplish when you are in the air. Then pack carefully to be sure that you have everything you need to make it a valuable flight.

When you fly, get to the airport early, 60 minutes before your flight departs. This will enable you to board your flight completely relaxed, with your mind calm and clear. You will be ready to begin working as soon as you are airborne.

GET RIGHT TO WORK

Once the plane takes off, you can lower your tray table, pull out your file, and begin working immediately. Resist the temptation to read the magazine in the pocket in front of you or watch the movies that they play on long flights. Don't drink alcohol of any kind. Instead, drink two glasses of water for every hour that you are in the air. This will keep you alert and refreshed and will dramatically cut down on jet lag.

One final rule for traveling: On the outbound leg of the flight, you should work on serious activities that require energy and concentration. Read books and magazines on the return flight when you are tired and not as sharp as you were earlier in the day.

In any case, make every minute count. Don't be like those people who drive around listening to the radio or who board the plane and either drink throughout the flight, watch the movie, or just sit there looking out the window. Turn your car into a mobile classroom and an airline seat into your flying office. Use them both to get ahead and stay ahead of your work.

GET BETTER AT YOUR KEY TASKS

This is one of the best time-management techniques of all. The better you get at the important things you do, the less time it takes you to complete them as well or better than before. The act of becoming very good at your key tasks can double your productivity. It can dramatically increase the quality and quantity of the work you get done and have an inordinate impact on your income.

Here's an example I use in my seminars. A person who types using the hunt-and-peck method (i.e., with the index fingers only) will type about five to eight words per minute. However, with a bit of practice, that same person can become a touch typist. With 30 minutes practice each day for 90 days, the average person can get his or her typing speed up to 5,080 words per minute.

Notice what has happened. In just three months, by getting better in this area, the person who was typing five to eight words per minute can now type 5,080 words per minute. This is an increase of ten times the output and productivity in the same amount of time.

COMMIT TO LIFELONG LEARNING

Getting better can have a major impact on the important things you do. If you sell for a living, dedicate yourself to becoming very good at prospecting, making presentations, and following up and closing the sale. If you are in management, commit yourself to becoming very good at selecting, delegating, supervising, and communicating with your key people.

Here is one of the most important questions you ever ask and answer: "What one skill, if you developed and practiced it consistently in an excellent fashion, would have the greatest positive impact on your career?'' If you don't know the answer to this question, go and ask your boss. Ask your co-workers. Ask your spouse. Ask your friends and customers. But you must find out the answer to this question.

Then, once you've identified the key skill, you write it down as a goal and set a deadline. Make a plan to acquire this skill and take action immediately. Then do something every day that moves you toward becoming absolutely excellent at the one thing you can do that can help you the most. This single time-management principle alone can change your life.

WORK IN REAL TIME

This is an extremely important principle for increasing your productivity. Develop a sense of urgency, a fast tempo. Develop a bias for action. Pick up the pace. Do it now!

Today, there is an incredible need for speed. People who do things quickly and well are considered to be smarter, more valuable, and more competent than people who do things slowly. Make decisions quickly. Fully 80 percent of decisions can be made the moment they come up. Don't delay or procrastinate on them. Slow decision-making simply plugs up your pipeline and puts a drag on your activities.

Complete all quick jobs as soon as they come up, as well. Anything that will take you less than two minutes is usually something that you should do immediately. Always think about how much time it will take you to ramp up and do the job later if you don't do it now.

Take an important phone call immediately and deal with it. Have an important discussion and make a decision to solve the problem right now. Respond to requests from your boss or your customers fast. Move quickly when need or opportunity arises. Develop a reputation for speed and dependability.

Your goal should be to develop a reputation for being the person who, when someone wants a job done fast, gets it done fast. This will open more doors for you than you can imagine. This will attract more opportunities to you to do more things quickly and well. Doing things quickly, when they come up, is a vital part of increasing your productivity.

REENGINEER YOUR WORK

This is one of the most popular and efficient ways to reduce time, energy, and expense in getting a job done. Most work processes and jobs today are multitask, multistep jobs.

As it happens, many of these jobs have evolved over time with many inefficiencies built in that no one really thinks about. Many steps are either unnecessary or actually useless. Nonetheless, they expand the amount of time it takes to do the job.

But this is not for you. Take any large task that you have to do and write down every single step necessary to complete that job from the initial idea to the finished task. Once you have a list of every single step, set a goal to reduce the number of steps by 30 percent the first time you go through the list. This is almost always possible when you use your creativity.

Look for ways to consolidate several steps into a single step. Look for ways to consolidate several jobs so that they are done by a single person at the same time. Look for ways to cut back, discontinue, or eliminate steps that are no longer necessary. Always ask, "Why are we doing it this way?" and "Could there be a *better* way?" Your ability to simplify and streamline your life and work so that you get more done in a shorter period of time is a major key to increasing your productivity.

REINVENT YOURSELF EACH YEAR

We are living at the time of the greatest change in all of human history. Things are changing so rapidly, in all areas, in all directions, that you must be continually reevaluating and reinventing yourself and your life. At least once a year, you should stand back and look at every aspect of your life to determine whether what you're doing is something that you want to continue doing.

Imagine for a moment that your company has burned to the ground and that you have to walk across the street and start over again in a new building. What would you start up immediately? What would you not start up at all? Who would you bring with you from the parking lot to continue working in your company? Who would you leave behind in the parking lot, if you had the choice?

Imagine that your job, your industry, and your business disappeared. Imagine that you were starting your career over again and you could go in any direction and do virtually anything. What would it be?

Evaluate where you live and how your family spends leisure time. Reevaluate your finances and your physical condition. If you could begin any part of your life and career over again, like a painter standing before a white canvas, how would you design or reinvent your life today?

When you stand back and look at your life from this point of view on a regular basis, you will begin to see all kinds of opportunities to change what you are doing so that they are more in line with what you really want. This is a real key to increasing your productivity and improving your life.

SET CLEAR POSTERIORITIES

You have heard of setting priorities. Priorities are tasks that you do more of and sooner. A *posteriority*, on the other hand, is something that you do less of and later, if at all.

The fact is that you are already overwhelmed with too much to do and too little time. For you to do something new or different, you must *discontinue* something that you are already doing. You must begin systematically setting posteriorities on activities in your life that are no longer as important as other activities. Practice "creative abandonment" with tasks and activities that are no longer as valuable as they were when you first started doing them.

You have too much to do already. Therefore, before you start something new, you have to stop doing something old. Picking up a new task requires putting down an old task. Getting in means getting out. Starting up means stopping off. Look at your life and your work. What sort of things should you stop doing so that you can free up enough time to do more of the things that you should be doing more of the time?

REGAINING CONTROL REQUIRES LETTING GO

You can only get your life under control to the degree to which you discontinue lower-value activities. You can only increase your productivity by freeing up more time to do the things that are more valuable and can have a significant payoff for you in the future.

When I get overloaded with work, I have a little motto that I repeat to myself: "All you can do is all you can do." Whenever you feel overloaded for any reason, whenever you feel that you have too much to do and too little time, stop, take a deep breath, and say to yourself, "All I can do is all I can do."

Then sit down, make a list of everything you have to do, and begin setting posteriorities on your time. Refuse to do anything that is not a good use of your time. Sometimes the word *no* can be the best time-saver of all.

KEEP YOUR LIFE IN BALANCE

The reason you are working should be that you can earn enough money to enjoy your family, your health, and the important parts of your personal life. You want to have happy, healthy, harmonious relationships with your spouse and children. You want to be healthy and fit. You want to grow, mentally and spiritually. You want to be as successful as possible in your work and your career so that you have the resources to do all the things that you really care about that have nothing to do with your work.

Unfortunately, most people get the cart before the horse. They become so preoccupied with their work that they lose sight of the reason for wanting to be successful at their work in the first place. This is definitely not for you.

Remember that in life, relationships are everything. Fully 85 percent of your success in life will come from your happy relationships with other people. Only 15 percent of your happiness will come from your achievements in your work or external activities. You must keep your life in balance.

SIMPLIFY AND IMPROVE YOUR LIFE

The keys to balance are simple. Set your peace of mind, your happiness, and your home life as your highest goals and organize the rest of your life around them. Create blocks of time to spend with your family. Create time in the evenings, time on the weekends, and time away on vacations. Remember the formula for balance: It is quantity of time at home that counts and quality of time at work. Don't mix them up.

The simplest of all rules for balance is to put people first. And of all the people whom you put first, put the most important people in your life ahead of everything and everyone else.

When you work, *work all the time you work.* Don't waste time with idle chit-chat and useless activities. Work all the time. Remember that every minute you waste at work with idle socializing is a minute that you are taking away from your family and your important relationships.

When you get your life in balance, you will actually accomplish more, be paid more, produce more, and have vastly more time with your family. This is the whole reason for wanting to become more productive in the first place.

BECOME INTENSELY ACTION-ORIENTED

Today, everyone is in a hurry. Your boss wants everything done immediately. Your customers did not even know they wanted your product or service until now, and now they want it yesterday. People are incredibly impatient. No one will wait in line anymore. The average Internet surfer will switch in seven to eight seconds if a website does not load quickly.

The most outwardly identifiable quality of the top performer, in every field, is that he or she is in constant motion. The top performer takes initiative to get the job done. The top performer takes action, over and over again, continuously toward the goal.

On the other hand, the greatest single obstacle to high performance is the tendency to talk a subject to death.

Many people think that talking well and planning continuously is the same as execution. But only action is action. Only execution is execution; only getting the job done really matters.

RESULTS ARE EVERYTHING

In the final analysis, you only get paid for results. Results are everything. Intense result-orientation goes hand in hand with high productivity and high performance in every area.

Make a decision today that you are going to move fast when an opportunity or need presents itself. Pick up the pace. Take action of some kind. Get on with it!

The good news is that the faster you move, the better you feel. The faster you move, the more energy you have. The faster you move, the more you get done. The faster you move, the more you learn and the more experience you get. And the faster you move, the more you get paid and the faster you get promoted.

THE FORMULA FOR HIGH PRODUCTIVITY

There is a basic five-step formula for getting the most out of yourself.

First, decide *exactly* what you want, in terms of your goals and objectives.

Second, make a *list* of everything that you have to do today to move you toward the achievement of those goals and objectives.

Third, organize your list by *priority* and select your A-1, the most important single task you could complete right now.

Fourth, begin immediately on your number-one task and discipline yourself to work at it single-mindedly until it is 100 percent complete.

Finally, keep repeating, over and over to yourself, the wonderful words, "Do it now! Do it now! Do it now!"

What Do You Do Now?

WE ARE LIVING in the greatest time in all of human history. There are no limits to what you can accomplish except for the limits that you place on yourself. Your job is to become one of the most productive people in your field. Your goal is to develop the reputation for being the person who, when anyone wants or needs something done, gets the job done.

Your job is to be one of the most productive and most valuable people in your business or organization. Your job is to get paid more and promoted faster. Your job is to have a wonderful life, and you do it by managing your time well and continually increasing your productivity. When you do this, you can become a great success at whatever you do at any point in your life. Reinventing yourself is easily within your grasp.

QUESTIONS FOR REFLECTION

1. Why are you on the payroll? Of all the things you've been hired to do, which one is most important?

2. What one skill, if you were absolutely excellent at it, would help you the most in your career?

3. What are some of the activities or tasks in your life that you should delegate, downsize, or eliminate?

4. If you could reinvent yourself today, with no limitations, what would you do differently?

5. What are the most important projects that you should get finished as soon as possible?

6. What are the things that only you can do that, if done well, can make a real difference in your work and personal life?

7. What are you going to start doing, or stop doing, immediately as the result of what you have learned in this book?

Brian Tracy is a professional speaker, trainer, and consultant and is the chairman of Brian Tracy International, a training and consulting company based in Solana Beach, California. He is also a self-made millionaire.

Brian learned his lessons the hard way. He left high school without graduating and worked as a laborer for several years. He washed dishes, stacked lumber, dug wells, worked in factories, and stacked hay bales on farms and ranches.

In his mid-twenties, he became a salesman and began climbing up through the business world. Year by year, studying and applying every idea, method, and technique he could find, he worked his way up to become chief operating officer of a $265–million development company.

In his thirties, he enrolled at the University of Alberta and earned a bachelor of commerce degree; then he earned a masters in business administration from Andrew Jackson University. Over the years, he has worked in twenty-two different companies and industries. In 1981, he began teaching his success principles in talks and seminars around the country. Today, his books, audio programs, and video seminars have been translated into thirty-five languages and are used in fifty-two countries.

Brian has shared his ideas with more than 4 million people in forty-five countries since he began speaking professionally. He has served as a consultant and trainer for more than 1,000 corporations. He has lived and practiced every principle in this book. He has taken himself and countless thousands of other people from frustration and underachievement to prosperity and success.

Brian Tracy calls himself an "eclectic reader." He considers himself not an academic researcher but a synthesizer of information. Each year he spends hundreds of hours reading a wide variety of newspapers, magazines, books, and other materials. In addition, he listens to many hours of audio programs, attends countless seminars, and watches numerous videotapes on sub-jects of interest to him. Information gleaned from radio, television, and other media also adds to his knowledge base.

Brian assimilates ideas and information based on his own expe-rience and that of others and incorporates them into his own expe-rience. He is the bestselling author of more than forty books, including *Maximum Achievement, Advanced Selling Strategies, Focal Point,* and *The 100 Absolutely Unbreakable Laws of Busi-ness Success.* He has written and produced more than 300 audio and video learning programs that are used worldwide.

Brian is happily married and has four children. He lives on a golf course in San Diego. He travels and speaks more than 100 times each year and has business operations in seventeen coun-tries. He is considered to be one of the foremost authorities on success and achievement in the world.

Brian Tracy is one of the top professional speakers in the world, addressing more than 250,000 people each year throughout the United States, Europe, Asia, and Australia.

Brian's keynote speeches, talks, and seminars are described as "inspiring, entertaining, informative, and motivational." His audiences include Fortune 500 companies and every size of business and association.

Call today for full information on booking Brian to speak at your next meeting or conference.

21st Century Thinking—How to outthink, outplan, and outstrategize your competition and get superior results in a turbulent, fast-changing business environment.

Advanced Selling Strategies—How to outthink, outperform, and outsell your competition using the most advanced strategies and tactics known to modern selling.

The Psychology of Success—How the top people think and act in every area of personal and business life.

Countless practical, proven methods and strategies for peak performance.

Leadership in the New Millennium—How to apply the most powerful leadership principles ever discovered to manage, motivate, and get better results, faster than ever before.

Brian will carefully customize his talk for you and for your needs. Visit Brian Tracy International at www.briantracy.com for more information, or call 858-481-2977 today for a free promotional package.